What the Reviewers Are Saying

David Womack's new book meets a real need in the field of church growth and literature. It is written with the layman in mind and presents the concepts of church growth without the technical jargon characteristic of most such books.

—The Alliance Witness

Though this pyramid principle is the heart of the book, it is by no means the only principle set forth.

He concludes with an exciting possibility for any church that grows beyond 1,200 members and still wants to remain effective. Though this vision is for the few, everything leading up to it is applicable to any church surrounded by unchurched people. If you read this book you won't be disappointed.

—His Dominion Magazine

Congregations who will catch the vision and apply the principle of this book will grow. A must for pastors and directors of Christian education as well as all concerned lay people.

—Christian Review

To read this book is to stimulate your thinking with fresh ideas. The local church which cannot get beyond the barrier of a small attendance needs its message.

—Pentecostal Evangel

THE PYRAMID PRINCIPLE
of Church Growth
David A. Womack

Bethany Fellowship INC.
MINNEAPOLIS, MINNESOTA 55438

· Published by Bethany Fellowship, Inc.
6820 Auto Club Road, Minneapolis, Minnesota 55438

Printed in the United States of America

Library of Congress Cataloging in Publication Data:

Womack, David A
    The pyramid principle.

    1. Church growth. I. Title.
BV652.25.W65   254'.5   76-46312
    ISBN 0-87123-462-9

*To Barbara, Joyce, and Carol
—my wife and daughters*

DAVID A. WOMACK is home secretary of the Assemblies of God Division of Foreign Missions. He and his editorial staff publish *Good News Crusades* magazine and provide missions material for the *Pentecostal Evangel*.

Rev. Womack is himself a former missionary, speaks Spanish fluently and has travelled the world extensively. He is also a producer of foreign missions films and author of three previous books. His eloquent appeal for all-out world evangelism, *Breaking the Stained-Glass Barrier*, was a selection of the Church Growth Book Club and was featured in *Christianity Today*.

A graduate of Northwest College (B.A. and M.A. in theology), an experienced pastor, and a church-planter in Colombia, Rev. Womack is amply qualified to write *The Pyramid Principle* as a layman's guide to church growth.

Preface

I once knew a man who had calluses on his knees. His name was Jim Evers, but to everyone in our street-meeting group he was "Brother" Evers. I would play my guitar to help gather a crowd so he could preach and wave his ragged-edged Bible.

At the end of most of our street meetings, he would lead someone along the street to the local mission, where he would soon have the fellow repenting of his sins. One day he asked the Lord to make it stop raining so we could continue our street meeting, and to my surprise the rain stopped!

As a youth, I was amazed at the man. He seemed to break all the laws of nature. So, I asked him what was the source of his power. That was when he showed me the calluses on his knees.

Many years have passed since I left the street corners of Spokane, Washington. Ironically, as I think of it now, I went away to theology school to learn how to do God's work. There in the isolation of such training I moved far from the men I had known in the streets. The experience of pastoring several American churches further separated me from the unchurched.

I took my wife and daughters to Colombia, South America, where as foreign missionaries we tried to fight Goliath in the armor of King Saul. We did what we were trained to do, but the people did not come inside the church to see us do it. We were warned we could be stoned or jailed if we took the gospel into the streets, but we reverted to the tactics of Brother Evers.

The predictions were true. Rocks were thrown at us, some of our people were wounded, and on one occasion I was arrested for preaching—but the churches began to grow! Before leaving Colombia for my present duties, we pastored Bogota's *Templo Bethel*, the largest Protestant church in the capital at that time. We had 800 to 1,000 people in our services, and our community outreach touched 2,000 to 3,000 others every Sunday in houses, parks, and in the streets.

I now serve as home secretary for the Assemblies of God Division of Foreign Missions—a worldwide missionary program whose number of members and adherents has doubled in the past 6 years, tripled in 12 years, and quadrupled in 16 years. It currently is adding more than 500,000 converts to the church each year.

My purpose in writing this book is to offer to the American churches some of the philosophies and methods of church growth that make possible the phenomenal successes of evangelical missions overseas.

I am an incurable fanatic, a hopelessly convinced propagandist whose belief in the necessity of continuous church growth has changed little since my street-meeting days. I believe that each church should continue to make converts and grow as long as there remains any unrighteousness in its community and its world.

I write this book for those Christian laymen who share with me in this concern that their local churches should continue to grow and for those pastors who are not satisfied with the separation of church and society.

Somewhere, perhaps only waiting for the call to action, there is a remnant of believers in open evangelization that is ready to break into creative, dynamic approaches to the spreading of apostolic Christianity.

Brother Evers, we miss you on the streets of our cities.

David A. Womack

Contents

1

The Joshua Predicament

Across my desk I looked into the troubled eyes of a pastor who had come to see me on his way home from a conference on church growth. His reaction was quite different from that of some of my nonpastor friends who had attended the meetings. Most had been warmly enthusiastic.

"The problem with the church-growth concepts," he was saying, "is that these modern ideas don't get to the laymen. If an idea doesn't reach the pulpit and the pew, you may as well forget it."

I agreed. Today's pastors are often exposed to the new church-growth ideas through religious magazines, books, seminars, and college courses. There even is a church-growth book club. But there is little on church growth for the laymen. I responded, "You know, Joshua faced that same predicament three thousand years ago."

His eyebrows raised. "Joshua had a problem with laymen?"

The explanation I gave him I shortly will share with you.

From that conversation and many other open talks with people all over the country, I came to realize the great gap in understanding of church growth between pastors and most Christians in the pew. Yet, the growth of a church must result from a cooperative effort involving all members of a congregation. I set out to write a book on church growth that pastors could share with interested laymen.

What resulted from my study was a little frightening because it questioned my own previous views and made me admit that today's church methods are inadequate for the late 20th century. Present styles are too expensive, too limited, and too slow. We must change our traditional concepts of church size and church strategy if we are to meet the challenge of our times. Such a change will require more than inspired and enthusiastic pastors; it will call for a creative vision among the Christian laymen.

New ideas do not come easily, but once they can be put into some sensible form they spread widely. Yet, no one really knows the source of new ideas. Some forgotten genius discovered that by chipping a stone he could form a cutting edge, and his idea formed the working model for the tools of thousands of generations. Another innovator brought fire under control, and he changed the way of life for the whole human race. Great new thoughts come rarely to man; but once a fresh idea is born it forms the basis for a new period of history.

Many Christians with a vision of what the church ought to be feel it is time to open our stained-glass windows and let in some fresh concepts. If the church is to accomplish its divinely appointed task, each congregation must attain a pattern of continuous growth. No church must ever stop growing, no matter what its size.

One of the most creative ideas of all time was the invention of the pyramid. Square at the bottom and pointed at the top, it was one of the wonders of the ancient world. Once someone had discovered its basic simplicity of design and built a prototype, the idea provided both the Egyptians and the Mayas with a characteristic feature of their cultures.

Fortunately, we think we know who built the first Egyptian pyramid. He was Imhotep, history's first engineer and constructor in stone. Imhotep designed and built the first large stone structure—the famous Step Pyramid at Sakkarah, Egypt. We probably never will know where he got his new idea some 5,000 years ago, but we do know that his terraced pyramid provided the concept for the other larger pyramids that were to follow. Imhotep's creative idea formed the basis for the many kinds of stone buildings that other men would develop through the ages from the Greek temples to the medieval cathedrals to the modern skyscrapers.

The time has come for a new idea in the church. We have pushed to its practical limits the medieval concept of building-centered church life. Now, if we are to fulfill the original design of the Body of Christ in the world, we must look for creative ways to attain continuous church growth.

The principle involved in producing such growth is like that of enlarging a pyramid. We may imagine Imhotep planning his Step Pyramid by stacking three stone slabs to make a scale model. He probably liked the idea, but he wanted to make the structure larger. What should he do—add another slab to the top? No! He was thinking in bigger terms, not smaller. He must have added another larger slab underneath his scale model. Finally, he stacked larger and larger bottom slabs until he had put together the six-terrace plan for his great structure. When finished, the pyramid measured 413 feet by 344 feet at the base and pointed some 200 feet into the heavens. To make a pyramid larger, you must enlarge its base and then add to its mass.

For a church to grow, it must follow much the same procedure, because a church grows only until it reaches the conceptual limitations of its pastor and congregation. If a church wishes to serve more people, it must first expand its base of organization and ministry. Only then may it add to its numerical mass of followers.

By pointing out the Pyramid Principle of church growth I emphasize the dynamic relationship between the base of church efficiency and the mass of congregational size. A church cannot grow beyond its own ability to care for a determined number of people. Therefore, for a church to grow it must first expand its base of operations.

It is difficult to recognize our own limitations. Yet, if we think about our goals, are willing to accept change, and ask the Lord for His guidance, we can begin to see where the next changes need to occur.

Sometimes human insight into the condition of the church comes about by some apparently absurd or unrelated event. I once experienced such a revelation in Ouahigouya, Upper Volta. In fact, the sight before my eyes on that West African day caught me embarrassingly unprepared for its ironic impact on my consciousness.

There, sitting hunch-winged on top of a church, was a big, black buzzard!

The world never has lacked for dead churches, but this was the ultimate in ecclesiastical mortification. Furthermore, the ugly scavenger did not speak well for my own ministry; just the night before, I had preached in that church!

Really, the church was not as dead as that unwelcome guest would have had me believe. The people were friendly. They supported their own pastor and paid their church expenses from their tithes and offerings. The congregation filled most of the seats in the sanctuary each Sunday. Except for the presence of my portentous friend on the roof—who kept reminding me of Edgar Allan Poe's "stately Raven of the saintly days of yore"—the church was much like any church anywhere in the world.

While I stood there dismayed by the enigmatic buzzard, who glared down at me like some stone gargoyle from the sculptured parapet of a medieval cathedral, I asked myself; *How can we reach this town?*

The answer was simple, although it was not immediately obvious to anyone who looked only upon the physical church building or attended only a few services. The evangelization of Ouahigouya would have to happen outside the walls of the church sanctuary.

Yes, that was the answer! It was not remarkably profound, but a new decision based on the idea of carrying the work of the congregation outside the church walls would revolutionize the ministry of the church in that community. In fact, the Upper Volta church is one of the fastest growing in the world.

The way to reach any community is to send into the streets the lay people in whose lives God has performed His miracles of salvation and personal guidance. True evangelization does not occur inside church walls, but out in the streets, on the jobs, and in the houses throughout the community.

Wherever I have traveled around the world I have found the same problems I observed in that African church. New churches grow for a while, then level off after they form their first nucleus of believers. This first stage often occurs between 35 and 50 in the Sunday school, and many churches never go beyond that point. After establishing its identity, a congregation may continue to grow; but it will tend to stabilize its expansion at predictable numerical sizes.

I once wrote that churches tend to level off their growth at 35, 85, 125, 180, 240, 280, 400, 600, 800, and just under 1,200. George Edgerly, a statistician with the Assemblies of God Sunday School Department, questioned my figures, so I asked him to analyze actual records and find out whether churches tend to stop growing at predictable sizes. Basing his analysis on a large national sample, Mr. Edgerly discovered that actual church sizes clustered about 50, 90, 120, 180, 230, 290, and 400. There were too few churches in the larger categories to establish a pattern. The size-frequency graph showed definite peaks at these levels and just as marked declines between the common clusters. For a nonmathematician, I had not missed the cluster points by far.

In my opinion, once a church is large enough to care for its own members, pay its own expenses, and establish a favorable image in the community, the congregation often loses momentum and is lulled into the peaceful slumber of religious passivity.

As I told that pastor in my office, I call this condition the Joshua Predicament.

I have taken this term from the problem faced in Israel after the conquest of Canaan. Moses had brought the Children of Israel out of Egyptian bondage and guided them through the difficult years in the Wilderness; but it was the younger Joshua who commanded the army and finally led the people into the Promised Land. City after city fell to the mighty conquerors who came so dedicated and strong out of the desert.

But a strange thing happened to the Israelites. Once they had conquered enough land for their immediate use, they stopped fighting. Men of war laid down the sword and took up the plowshare and sickle. The fiery-eyed fighters from the desert became the well-fed farmers of a land flowing with milk and honey.

Something similar happens to many churches. They rise in a flame of glory; but once they grow large enough to take care of their own immediate needs, they tend to level off their initial activities and growth. They put community evangelization aside as their hands take up other tasks related to their internal congregation development.

This is the negative side of the Pyramid Principle. If a church ceases to expand its base of administration and ministry, it stops growing.

God was not happy with the Israelites' failure to occupy the whole Promised Land. In fact, much of Israel's trouble since that time appears to have resulted from its diminutive size. The initial mistake of not establishing a larger base determined from the beginning that neighboring armies would overrun the country time after time.

The Bible says in Joshua 13:1: *"Now Joshua was old*

and stricken in years; and the Lord said unto him, Thou art old and stricken in years, and there remaineth yet very much land to be possessed."

The condition I have called the Joshua Predicament was that Joshua ran out of time and momentum before he finished his God-given task. The Lord had demanded the total occupation of the Promised Land, not just a token presence of Israel in Canaan; but the leaders were old and tired and ready to settle down short of fulfilling their destiny.

Today, we face the problem of an aging church and an unfinished task. As God called for the total occupation of the Promised Land, so He now calls for the total evangelization of the world. Jesus said, "Go ye therefore, and teach all nations" (Matt. 28:19). Yet, many churches lie bound in the chains of medieval traditions and static leadership, tired and out of ideas at a time when they need to be at their conquering best. Old and stricken in years, they suffer from what some have called "hardening of the categories."

It takes a tremendous burst of power to break inertia and develop new momentum for any task. This is particularly true for the church, for we have accumulated many nonessential traditions over the centuries.

The church is like a junk dealer's cart that on its trip through history has gathered such a clutter of obsolete relics that it breaks down under the weight of its own antiquated load. If we are ever to repair the junk dealer's cart and get it rolling again, we must remove the load of useless clutter that broke it down in the first place. A certain nostalgic appreciation for the past is necessary for the accurate interpretation of the present; but we must not allow traditions to continue if they do not apply to the present. History is a nice place to visit, but we should not live there.

One of the most ironic lessons of the past is that although the church ought to be a moving, creative, alternative-seeking influence in the world, in practice it has become the most conservative, unyielding, traditional enterprise in our society. Instead of daring imagination and responsible leadership, the church offers only a cautious pessimism. It has a reputation of pointing out old paths in a new forest, while the real need of the world is for courageous trailblazers who will lead the way safely through the unfamiliar foliage of the present.

Must we scrap the junk dealer's cart and build a new vehicle?

Some people call for a new kind of church put together from the bits and pieces from breaking down the differences between religious groups. They would remove all the objectionable "distinctives" of the churches and combine what would be left into a single ecumenical system. The word for such a mixing of various religious beliefs into one credal system is *syncretism*. The unfortunate mixture of foreign ideas into the once pure essence of original apostolic Christianity has been responsible for much of the deterioration of the church. There is nothing to be gained by pooling the weaker characteristics of many ineffective churches, for the huddling together of a lot of cold congregations will not produce a single warm one.

Diversification is the true sign of life, not unification. As many forms of life will fill the ecological niches in an environment, so different kinds of churches will reach into the very complex socio-cultural environment of a community. The church does not need to be replaced by any new religious system. What it needs is to reach all the way back to its own apostolic origins and be reborn to a new creative life.

We may consider a local church in one of three ways: history-oriented, self-oriented, or task-oriented. To put it another way, a church worker may consider himself a museum curator who maintains the church in memory of the past, a short-order cook who cares only for the current requests of his present customers, or a conqueror who lays a strategy for total victory and pursues his dream as a man of destiny.

The tragedy of the Joshua Predicament was that while Israel's leader was old and stricken in years, there yet remained much land to be possessed. Joshua ran out of momentum before he ran out of territory to conquer. Many of today's churches have fallen into the same condition, for they seem more intent on establishing a token presence in each community than on pressing onward to total world evangelization. Surrounded by millions of unchurched and unevangelized people, such churches go on year after year with few converts and little change in their numerical size. What a tragedy that they should be out of energy at such a crucial moment in history!

God's solution to the Joshua Predicament was that the land should be divided into tribal inheritances so the task could be entrusted to a broader base of lay leaders. The Lord said to Joshua (13:7-8): "*Now therefore divide this land for an inheritance unto the nine tribes, and the half tribe of Manasseh, with whom the Reubenites and the Gadites have received their inheritance, which Moses gave them, beyond Jordan eastward.*"

God told Joshua to decentralize the responsibility and divide the task among the common people. Great men call for new concepts at the turning points of history, but the continued vitality of any organization will rise or fall with its degree of popular participation. No operation that intends to pervade a community can accomplish its goals without the willing cooperation of many people. By decentralizing responsibility and involving a greater number of laymen in evangelistic action, a church may recapture its vitality and move into a pattern of continuous growth.

As long as the Children of Israel marched on the hot sands of the desert they could rally around men like Moses and Joshua; but once they got their plows into the soil and began to raise their children on captured land, they had to have more than old warrior-prophet leaders to inspire them to conquest. This is one of the secrets of church growth— to keep the base of activity and leadership broad enough to involve all the people at different levels of church life.

It takes a depth of vitality and involvement to keep a church alive and growing. Leadership only from the top of an organization will ultimately stifle growth and extinguish life. Leaders must draw on the potential vitality of the whole body and motivate all cells, organs, and systems to function in a healthy and coordinated manner. By delegating authority and motivating large numbers of dedicated laymen, leaders may produce massive centralized results. There is not a church in the world that cannot grow by adopting these principles. There is an almost limitless potential for growth in a congregation of Christian laymen if a church can unleash the power of each individual and direct lay energy into a meaningful pattern of progress.

The question is whether a congregation will dare to unlatch the door of unpredictable creativity. Will a board of deacons be willing to allow new converts to upset its power balance? Will the social structure of the church admit new members as readily as the ministerial staff takes them in? Can a basically conservative pastor muster the courage to surround himself with creative, activated laymen? There is little point in pursuing the subject of church growth if the pastor, board, and congregation are not prepared to assimilate new people into their midst.

Yet another lesson we may learn from God's instructions to Joshua is that by dividing the task among the tribes Joshua would increase his points of engagement with the enemy and thus multiply his chances of success.

A local church must consider its points of engagement with the community. A normal congregation contacts its surrounding population first by its church building. The material facilities are not the most important contact with the unchurched, but they are the most easily recognized.

Ask anyone in town if he has heard of your church, and he will probably tell you its location. He thinks it is a place, not a body of people. This identification of the church as a building is a very limited view, but it is a basic concept with most people.

A church also contacts its community by its reputation —its public image. The residents of a town attach to their mental picture of the church a good, bad, or indifferent attitude based on their own experience and on rumors. For this reason, a church must learn to build its own public image for the best possible influence.

Another point of engagement is the minister's relationship to the community. The pastor may be a reclusive person who keeps his congregation between himself and the outside world, or he may be the extroverted type who shows up for every public occasion. Whatever the pastor's personality, the ministers on the staff may exert a positive influence on the town if they will understand their role in the community and take advantage of their opportunities.

The greatest potential influence of the church comes from the congregation itself. Everyone in regular or even erratic attendance is a point of engagement with the community. If properly motivated, trained, and mobilized for action, the laymen may become an irresistible force for evangelism.

Most unchurched people in America do not refrain from church attendance because of any real ideological disagreement with Christianity; rather, they are nonreligious by habit. Just as the church separates itself from the world by its traditions, so unchurched people separate themselves from the church because they never have conceived of themselves as religious people. If the church will break its old habits and approach men in new paths, it may influence unchurched people to change their life-styles as well. Church growth results from an aggressive program that keeps the whole congregation on the offensive, influencing the surrounding population for Christ and adding new converts to the church.

How large should a local church become?

No matter whether it numbers 35 people or 3,500, no congregation dedicated to the total evangelization of its community and world can ever stop adding converts. The larger the church becomes, the wider the scale of its potential operation and the more it may accomplish for Christ. No church of any size should ever stop growing,

Yet, many churches face the difficult challenge of the Joshua Predicament. Old and stricken in years, they are so bound in yesterday's traditions that they are incapable of realistic adaptation to this kind of Christianity. God's answer to Joshua still is the best response to this problem: *Decentralize the church programs to involve as many dedicated laymen as possible, and seek to expand the points of engagement with the community for a task-oriented approach to evangelism.* This ancient advice to an early leader of God's people still stands in the late 20th century.

One secret of church growth is what I have called the Pyramid Principle. Before a church may add to its mass of members and adherents it must expand its base of organization and ministry. Only by maintaining a dynamic relationship between numerical growth and administrative structure may a church develop a pattern of continuous expansion. To put it more simply, a church will not grow beyond its ability to care for its people.

We must get that vulture off our steeple and revitalize the church for its divine task in the world.

2

Church at the Boiling Point

A ray of golden sunlight beamed through the stained-glass windows and burst into a myriad of color across the empty pews of the church where I had been a guest missionary speaker. Now it was Monday—bleak, lonely Monday, when the mind of the minister is drained of all the clever lines that graced Sunday's sermons, and the sanctuary that yesterday was filled with praise now echoes to the sound of our footsteps.

The pastor and I went to the front of the sanctuary, where I sat on the first pew and he paced nervously beside the altar rail. I felt sorry for him. He had expected me to tell his laymen about the progress of the church in other lands, but I had gone beyond his expectations to challenge his congregation to missionary action in their own community. The people had responded warmly as if only waiting for someone to signal the beginning of a new restoration of apostolic Christianity.

"That's what I don't understand," the pastor told me. "In the services they act as though they want to reach the whole world, but afterward I can't get any cooperation from them. I want my church to grow, but frankly I don't know how to motivate these laymen."

I looked around at the impressive sanctuary with its expensive furniture, its beautiful tapestries, and its massive stained-glass windows. The church had been less than filled on Sunday, although it had enough people to give the appearance of a normal, fairly popular congregation. I told him, "Maybe they want their church to grow, but just aren't able to project themselves into the picture."

He shook his head. "I can't even get enough Sunday school teachers, far less move to a larger expansion. You should see the enthusiasm I get when I announce a visitation night. It's absolute zero . . . nothing."

I remembered the poor greeting I had received when I arrived at the church on Sunday morning. The ushers had not been on duty during the Sunday school hour, so there was no one at the door to welcome strangers. I had stood there awkwardly for a moment, wondering which door to take next. It would have been a frightening experience for anyone not accustomed to the series of barriers that worshipers place between themselves and the outside world; but as a missionary speaker I was used to confronting some variation of this obstacle course on most Sunday mornings.

I had made my way through the busy hubbub of the vestibule and entered the sanctuary, where a Sunday school class had just begun. A little old lady came up to me and pressed a slip of paper into my hand. It was an attendance form asking for my name and address, wanting to know if I was a member of the class, and offering me 100 points if I arrived on time, studied my lesson, gave money, and brought a Bible. No one told me whether there were other adult classes, so I sat in the rear of the sanctuary and listened to a man who ignored the lesson I was supposed to have studied and told how somebody had questioned his faith that week and how he had set the fellow straight. Most of the class members arrived late, but still they got to meet the little old lady and have an attendance slip placed into their eager hands.

The morning service had been good, but very predictable. There was an opening prayer, followed by a couple of hymns not related to the missionary theme of the service, a prayer for the unspecified needs of the congregation, a public reading of the announcements already printed in the bulletin, an offering, and a choir anthem. Finally, I had been introduced to speak. The people responded conservatively—not too loudly, not too fervently, with just the right degree of religious conviction taught them since childhood. It was a very normal church with a congregation of very nice people. They had no enemies and made few new friends.

I asked the pastor, "Do the laymen know your goals?"

"Sure," he said. "Our goals are those of any church. We worship God and teach His Word. We offer a good environment for fellowship among our adults, and good activities for our children and young people. We built this church about five years ago. Before that, we were downtown in an old building where the congregation had met for thirty years."

"But that could be the story of almost any church in America," I objected. "What are your goals for a year from now? What do you want your church to be like five years from now? Do you have a plan for the future?"

He looked at the sunlight through a blood-red pane of glass, and when he turned back to look at me he had an expression of frustration that ministers seldom allow themselves to bring to the surface. "Yes," he said with deep feeling in his voice, "I know I should organize, set goals, plan to take the whole city for Christ. You don't have to tell me that. I once had big plans for this church, but I can't move these people! I've tried, believe me, but they just don't respond past a certain point. I finally settled for moving the church to a better part of town and building a new sanctuary."

It was the same story I had heard across America from hundreds of pastors. Most ministers know what to do with a growing church, but few know how to motivate their congregations to start the growth process. I told this pastor, "The pitiful thing is that your people are just as frustrated as you are. They want to belong to an active, growing church. They don't have any enthusiasm for the present program, but they've never seen any other pattern. They don't know how to be motivated, but if you will lead them out of this monotonous trap, they'll follow you."

"Just like that?" he asked skeptically. "All right, how do I start?"

It was the right question, but I knew no simple answer. Every pastor is different, as is every congregation. The question reminded me of a test question in theology school: Define the doctrine of the Trinity in 25 words or less! Yet, I had to give him something to break his church out of its frozen state and hopefully bring it to the boiling point. I said, "First, go into your pulpit next Sunday with the same feeling you have right now. Take with you a list of priorities for the next year, and growth figures you want to reach in the next six months. Name some committees to study how to raise the response level of the congregation, how to increase your involvement in foreign missions, and how to influence the local community. Choose your most active laymen for committee chairmen, and ask for written reports. Engage your young people in discussion groups on evangelism outside the church walls. Then, call a special business meeting and have each committee chairman speak on the finding of his committee. Announce that your midweek service for the next three months will be a training session for lay activities in the new format. Report your changes to the newspapers and local television stations so you commit yourselves to action."

He stared at me. "There's got to be more to it than that."

"There is," I agreed. "Every time you go into your pulpit, act as though you've got a thousand people out there. Prepare your whole program for what you want to attain, not for what you've already got. That's where faith comes in . . . 'the substance of things hoped for, the evidence of things not seen.' Faith always lives in the future."

Before we left the sanctuary that day, we knelt and prayed for growth in the church, courage for the pastor, and a group of willing laymen to cooperate with such a bold step of faith.

All across the country I have talked with pastors and laymen. I have preached in many hundreds of churches. I have seen certain patterns emerge. Some kinds of churches grow, while others remain static or decline. Certain attitudes and methods produce an increase in congregational size, while others do not. Many churches tend to level off at certain stages of growth, and there they remain unless they recognize their problems and restructure for the next stage of development. The signs become unmistakable.

I believe in church growth. No matter what the present size of a church, no congregation has a right to stop making converts as long as there remains even one person on earth who has not had a fair chance to know Jesus Christ.

The question is not whether a small church should grow large or whether a large church should grow larger; it is rather that any church of any size must continue to work at the task of total world evangelization. As long as the task is undone, there must be no such thing as a nongrowing church any more than there could be a nongrowing child.

There probably is not a mother alive who in some secret moment has not wished her little baby could always remain tiny and beautiful in her arms. Yet, if the slightest indication of arrested growth should appear, she would be the first to become alarmed at its abnormality. A child must grow, for it was born to develop into a mature, adult member of the human race.

Churches are supposed to grow, too. The Lord intended that His church would become a dynamic force in the world, converting the heathen and bringing Christian believers to full spiritual maturity. It is inconceivable that a group of people with the answer to the world's problems should retreat behind its own walls and be satisfied with the development and care of its own limited number of members. The mission of the church cannot be accomplished in isolation.

The Mossi tribesmen of Upper Volta, West Africa, have an interesting way of providing good grazing for their cattle. At the end of a long, hot dry season, they take a bunch of dry grass in their hands and set fire to it. Then, they shake falling fire onto the dead grass all over the countryside. Wherever the fire falls, the old grass is burned away so the new grass may grow. When the rainy season comes, the waters fall from the heavens, and the new green grass springs up from the African soil. The cattle eat again, and thus provide food for the whole community of men.

Something similar needs to happen in our churches all over the world. At the end of a long dry season, we need new life from heaven. We need to let new fire fall to burn away the dead traditions from yesterday's revivals. We need to let new ideas, new ways of doing things, and new showers of blessing come down from heaven. We need new growth so our churches will be large and vital enough to feed the spiritual needs of men.

Just as the Mossi fire spreads wherever it falls, so every church must grow wherever it is located. With more than four billion people in the world, it is unthinkable that any church anywhere would stop reaching out to the lost and bringing men into the life and love of God.

However, church growth in America is a difficult problem. There is in our country a religious phenomenon that we must understand if we are to have any comprehension of the condition of our churches. Early in our history, Americans reacted against the idea of a state church and therefore developed a strong preference for local congregational autonomy.

For example, in his *Theological Dictionary* (published by Joseph J. Woodward, Philadelphia: 1826, p. 94), Charles Buck said that "each congregation of Christians which meets in one place for religious worship is a complete church, and has sufficient power to act and perform everything relative to religious government within itself, and is in no respect subject or accountable to any other church."

This concept pervades religion in the United States. Americans not only believe in the separation of church and state; they believe in the separation of church and church. They like churches with a strongly individualized congregational identity. Even though most American churches are members of some denominational organization, there still runs vehemently through even the most highly structured denominations a fierce spirit of congregational independence. It may vary slightly from one group to another, but this social concept is present to some degree in every church in America.

In a typical community there are Protestant churches from each of the historical periods, each appropriately constructed and furnished in the suitable fashion in vogue at the time of its founding. Each will have modernized in some way, but the basic themes will prevail. There will be a European-style liturgical church, an early American colonial church, a freewill or predestinational version from one of the ante-bellum revival periods, a post-bellum holiness or missionary society church, and a 20th-century Pentecostal church. In addition, there may be some post-World War II independent or auxiliary operations outside the normal congregational mode, such as youth centers, coffee houses, or other socially oriented activities. Members of any of the above groups may also participate in the contemporary charismatic meetings in private homes, hotel conference rooms, and other places.

The spirit of competition between churches is a major problem in our country. Even congregations within the same denomination may bitterly oppose one another. If similar churches would agree on a unified strategy for reaching their communities, they would revolutionize American life.

Before we may find ways to make the American churches

grow, we need a clear definition of the ideal local church. I say "ideal" because I will describe the church as I wish it to become, not as I often experience it.

An ideal local church is an assembly of Christian believers united together and meeting in and around one location for the worship of God, the preservation and teaching of apostolic Christian doctrine and experience, the fellowship of believers, and the total evangelization of its community and world.

In the strictest sense, there is no such thing as a local church. Every church, even though located in one place, is a manifestation of the whole Body of Christ and therefore shares with all other churches in the responsibilities of the whole church. There is one Body of Christ in the world, and if any local congregation is to prosper it must identify itself with that Body and share in its task. The Body of Christ is not fragmented into local churches or even denominations, but exists in its entirety wherever it is manifested.

The biblical definition of the church as the Body of Christ necessarily infers the idea of growth. It is in the very nature of any living body to grow or deteriorate. In the first apostolic church "the Lord added to the church daily such as should be saved" (Acts 2:47). Within a short time "the number of disciples was multiplied" (Acts 6:1). There is no biblical justification for a nongrowing church.

The chronic illness of the church is lethargy. Slowed by the inertia of its own conservative traditions, the church loses momentum and levels off its activity to the bare minimum required to pay its debts and care for its own members. Jesus said of such churches, "I know thy works, that thou art neither cold nor hot: I would thou wert cold or hot. So then because thou art lukewarm, and neither cold nor hot, I will spue thee out of my mouth" (Rev. 3:14-16).

It is not difficult to identify a cold or lukewarm church, for its symptoms are as obvious as those of the common cold. Once the chill factors set in, there will be a low level of enthusiasm in the pulpit and pew, characterized by the absence of a sense of expectancy. Hearing problems develop, for the lukewarm to cold congregation ceases to respond to the preacher in the normal manner of an audience with a speaker. As the minister tires of waiting for a response from his congregation of nonhearers, he retreats to expository sermons and the telling of Bible stories without applying the scriptural truths to the lives of his people. Productive work diminishes as the flow of new converts declines or disappears altogether, and in its place come many busy substitute activities that offer only an illusion of accomplishment. Worship becomes perfunctory, as bland for its lack of heartfelt praise as cold broth without salt.

Rated between 1 and 10 on a formality/informality scale, a problem church is either in the chilling 1-to-3 range of cold formality or in the feverish 8-to-10 range of extreme informality. To put it more simply, the patient may don a black tie and tuxedo, lift his nose in the air, and pretend he has nothing wrong with him; or, he may wrap himself in a bathrobe, hug a hot-water bottle, and sit with his feet in a basin of steaming water and Epsom salts. No matter which the response, the same infirmity is common to them both.

All healthy churches will not react to successful vitality in the same way, nor will they reach the same classes of people. Before we decide to judge churches for their styles of worship, we must allow for a wide divergence of cultures, social identifications, historical developments, and individual preferences. Still, on a formality/informality scale of 10, they will tend toward the middle 4-to-7 range of normal human response. Churches with an inclination toward formal worship will yet be friendly and open to receive strangers into their numbers. While insisting upon order in their acts of worship, they will allow their sense of religious wonder to expand into spontaneous praise.

Those who prefer an informal style will still retain a feeling of praise as an act of worship and will remain tolerant of those who sincerely do not appreciate religious informality. They will not become so loose in their attempt at common popularity that they neglect good planning and preparation, nor will they allow their down-home talk to degenerate into sacrilege. The man who announced his Sunday night service as "an old-fashioned Holy Ghost gully-washer" may have gone too far.

One very accurate way to take the temperature of a congregation is to observe where the people sit. In the lukewarm to cold churches the people generally sit toward the rear of the sanctuary, leaving a secure space between themselves and the pulpit. As the temperature rises, the congregation moves slowly, if reluctantly, toward the front, much as the mercury climbs in a thermometer.

For a church to grow it must increase its level of intensity. All boredom must be eliminated, and in its place must come a sense of expectancy that neither expends itself in cheap emotionalism nor dissipates into a fog of mysticism. It must be a purposeful attitude of wonder at what God is doing in the church and gratitude to God for the privilege of participating in His work.

Herein lies the fundamental problem of church growth—how to raise the temperature of a cold church and transform it into a warm and expanding body of true Christian believers. Whatever its historical development or cultural pattern, any church that sincerely identifies itself with apostolic Christianity with its doctrines, religious experiences, practices, and priorities can become a wonderfully warm expression of God's love and grace to its whole community.

However, something more is needed than a sense of well-being and a condition of increasing numbers. The massive spiritual needs of our times demand that the church go into an unprecedented period of growth. Warmth of heart is not enough; the church must now be heated to the boiling point. It must expand into a fervent evangelistic force in the world, bubbling over with inspired enthusiasm and filling every community with its fiery message of hope and salvation.

There is an old proverb that says, "A watched pot never boils."

Actually, it is not true, for it is intended to teach us a lesson about human impatience, not the effect of human eyesight on the boiling process. It only appears that it won't boil because the watcher cannot predict exactly when the pot will start to bubble.

The boiling of water at sea level is 212 degrees Fahrenheit. If you apply sufficient heat to the bottom of a pot of water, it must eventually come to the boiling point whether or not you watch it. It is a natural law. To be able to predict the exact moment of boiling, you would have to know the intensity of the heat, the nature and thickness of the pot, and the amount and previous temperature of the water. In fact, the water probably would boil away before you could figure it out.

It is just as difficult to determine when a church will reach the boiling point. As we watch it with deep concern, it may seem as though it never will respond. But, there are spiritual laws at work that must one day start the process if the heat is applied. Somewhere, if we raise the level of intensity in the congregation, there is a boiling point when a church with the right combination of factors has to start growing.

The question is whether the causative conditions can be created, or if one has to wait for them to happen spontaneously. The bubbles in a boiling pot may seem spontaneous, but they result from the purposeful application of heat to the pot. There are things that a congregation may do to bring their church to a condition of growth. We must pursue those things and apply them to each congregation.

A major problem in many American churches is that they are too far removed from the flame of original, apostolic Christianity. Rather than handling directly the realities of apostolic religion, they use symbols for the New Testament values. In effect, such churches are like ceremonial pots on a ritual fire, and they never, never boil.

There are other churches whose congregations are just waiting for someone to sound the call to action. True church growth awaits those courageous people who will dare to place the pot of their church over the flame of apostolic Christianity and see what happens.

3
The Jericho March

The jet plane came in low over the rooftops of Chicago's west side and settled down on one of the runways of O'Hare International Airport. Moments later, a pastor met me at the baggage claim area and led me out to his car in the parking lot. I was to speak for his missions convention.

We talked of the inevitable subjects that always come up between airport and church—how the church was doing, what the plans were for the weekend, when and for what groups I would be speaking, and how much the church had given to foreign missions during the previous year.

We were driving in a multi-lane stream of heavy traffic, and on both sides of the wide freeway there were rows and rows of houses all crowded together as though the Midwest had run out of space. I could not help thinking how many thousands of people we already had passed by on our way to the church, for all about us were the signs of a large population.

The pastor was talking about a congregation of several hundred people, surrounded by a massive city of millions; yet I knew that the combined churches of greater Chicago were reaching only a small percentage of the Windy City.

I asked him, "What is our overall strategy for reaching Chicago?"

He did not seem prepared for such a question, so I rephrased it. "Have there been any meetings to lay out a general plan for evangelizing the whole city?"

He shook his head and replied, "If there have been, I wasn't invited. There are some ecumenical meetings, but they don't try to evangelize a community. They want to blend with other ideas, not convert people to Christ in the apostolic manner. I guess each church just carries on its own program."

"But no one church can evangelize all of Chicago," I said. "Doesn't it make sense that you should at least get together with other churches of your own type and develop a strategy for the city?"

He smiled as though I did not understand what it is like to pastor a church in Chicago. "This is a big city," he told me. "The key word here is competition. Every church competes with every other church for the attention of the people. You don't talk much with other pastors. If you're doing all right, then you don't need to talk with them. If you're not, then you don't want to let them know about it."

"So you settle for building up a congregation of four or five hundred people?" I asked.

He laughed. "Are you kidding? I'll be shouting glory when we can stay in the two hundreds! In a place like Chicago people are sick and tired of the hassle with the crowds. They don't want a big church. They want to escape from the rush they're in all week and worship God in seclusion with a small group of their friends. So, it's like an act of creation every time we get a new convert. Most of our new people are already converted, but come from some other part of the country or even from some other Chicago church. People are always getting mad at their pastor or somebody in their congregation, so they come to my church for a while until they get mad at me. That's the way it works in a large city."

It sounded cynical, but I knew he was telling me the truth. "That's very sad," I said. "But it seems to me that it's all the more reason for churches to work together. You're surrounded by millions of unchurched people, and yet you compete for the same roving congregation over and over again. If you could just put an end to the competition and begin to work together on a unified strategy, you could make a great impact on Chicago."

He grinned and said, "I guess your job allows you the luxury of being an idealist. It must be nice."

I started to tell him that when I was a pastor in Bogota, Colombia, other missionaries and I developed a local-church program that reached 3,000 to 4,000 people every Sunday, but I thought better of it. Instead, I just watched the heavy traffic go by, and wondered how many people between the airport and the church had never attended a gospel service in their whole lives.

The conversation I have just described is a composite of hundreds of similar exchanges I have had with pastors in major cities all over the United States. It is typical of the responses I have gotten in Los Angeles, New York, Kansas City, or Seattle. Not even my home city of Springfield, Missouri, has escaped my repeated question: *What is our overall strategy for reaching this city?*

I ask my favorite question often because I believe that the task of the church can be accomplished in America only if we put a stop to interchurch competition and begin to plan a unified strategy for the evangelization of every community in our country. By a unified strategy, I do not mean that any one church should give up its autonomy or that small churches should be swallowed up by the bigger ones. What I do mean is that the local churches must work together at the task of evangelizing their communities. No one church can possibly evangelize any one community alone; so it only seems reasonable that the alternative course is to carry out the task together, especially with other churches of similar doctrine and historical background.

The fact is that churches of the same denomination often do not work together. Two or more sister congregations tend to reach into the same economic groups in the community, so they enter a pattern of rather fierce competition, each claiming to be more spiritual, more sophisticated or more "country," or more conveniently located than the other. George MacDonald was right when he said, "Division has done more to hide Christ from the view of men than all the infidelity that has ever been spoken." If a denomination is to evangelize a community, it must first clean up its own house and present to the outside world a united front of Christian love and understanding. Internecine feuds between similar churches only weaken both congregations and drive away the potential converts who may not appreciate a spirit of competition in the house of God.

The competitive spirit in American churches has been learned more from commerce than from religion. The methods of private enterprise in the open market of American business, with their characteristic advertising and competitive price systems, have offered much to be admired in our culture; but we should not have adopted such ideas into the church. The product of the church is not a salable item manufactured better in some churches than in others. Our goal is not to rise above other churches and capture the market. Victory in one church is not the defeat of another. We are brothers—the sons of God on assignment to preach the gospel to a lost world. The difficulty of one church is a problem for us all, and the success of any church should be our common joy. Our spirit of competition is worse than a mere unwise practice; it is a sin.

When will we learn that every church has a unique personality and that it takes all kinds of churches to pervade a community with the gospel? Formal, informal, sophisticated, country, suburban, inner-city—all these churches reach different social groups. They don't compete with each other any more than two trains can run into one another on separate tracks! These differences are not weaknesses of the church; they are deep strengths that prove the message of Christ is applicable to any group of people on the face of the earth. Even if all churches would agree on doctrine, they would still divide into separate congregations over their dissimilarities in musical preferences, styles of dress, and economic strata. The diversification of churches is a healthy sign of vibrant life; it is not a problem if the churches do not insist that one kind of gospel-preaching church is better than another church that preaches and practices the same message.

The only proper excuse for the opposition of one church against another is the question of purity of apostolic doctrine. There is only one Christian religion—that which was established by Jesus Christ and taught to the world by His apostles in the first century. There are religious groups in our country that are not truly Christian in belief or in practice, and they must be considered as objects of Christian evangelization rather than brothers with whom we should cooperate. A church is truly Christian which identifies itself with the doctrines, the religious experiences, the practices, and the priorities of apostolic Christianity. Naturally, there must be room for some variations of interpretation of the New Testament writings; but these must be based on serious Bible exposition rather than resulting from the influence of non-Christian sources. A church ceases to be Christian in direct proportion to its variation from original apostolic standards.

Christianity is an exclusive religion. If Jesus Christ is God come in human flesh to reveal himself to us, and if the only way for men to reach God is through belief in and obedience to Jesus Christ; then, all who believe in non-Christian religions are wrong, and the followers of Jesus Christ must attempt to save such people from their deadly errors.

If the Christian religion is to pervade every community on earth with its message of salvation, then every local congregation must cooperate with others of like faith to accomplish the task. This calls for an end to interchurch competition and a new context of Christian cooperation. It means that each congregation must view its task in the context of the whole community rather than merely the nurture and protection of its own members and their families.

Yes, if the whole church is to accomplish its divine assignment in this generation, then all gospel-preaching congregations must work together on a unified strategy; but that is not all that needs to happen. This is only the tip of the iceberg compared with what else each congregation must do if it is to participate meaningfully as an evangelistic force in its community.

What most congregations are doing today, even when they work together with other groups of like faith, will at best establish only a token presence of the church in their communities, not the total evangelization that Christ has required of His followers. A token effort is not enough. The gospel must pervade every community on the face of the earth.

To orient itself to such a task, a congregation must change its whole attitude from one of secluded worship to that of open confrontation with society. This implies a complete rebirth to a new form of life. The once-crawling caterpillar must awaken from its long sleep, break from the protective bonds of its cocoon, and soar on the wind with the marvelous wings it was born to bear. Such is the metamorphosis that must occur to transform a congregation into a truly apostolic church.

I was discussing the problems of church growth with a Sunday school class in Texas, and I said the congregation needed to break out of the prison of its own concepts and escape to the realization of its apostolic potentials. It was not the best choice of words for a Sunday school class, for the purpose of language should always be clarity, not obfuscation.

One man, whom the pastor had previously introduced

to me as a good, old boy, lifted his hand and said, "Frankly, you're kind of hard to follow."

I immediately liked him for his embarrassed honesty. I said, "I've been told that before. Some people think church growth can only happen somewhere else."

"Well, now," he said, "that's what I was thinking. You said the church should be like a cate'pillar and turn into a butterfly. Well, that's all right if you've got the right kind of cate'pillar . . . but most of us can't do what you're talking about because we're just plain, ordinary moths."

It got a good laugh from the class, and I enjoyed it as much as they did. I said, "At least a moth doesn't just sit there acting like a caterpillar, but it gets busy doing what it was born to do. Even a common moth knows enough to follow the light. Any church can change its attitude about itself and its community."

A nicely dressed lady, who might have been a librarian or a fifth-grade teacher, asked, "What changes of attitude do you suggest?"

"First," I told her, "a congregation needs to change its attitude about itself. It must not see itself as a small, misunderstood minority, retreating to the seclusion of its sanctuary to talk in privacy with its God. Rather, it should see itself as a dedicated body of God's messengers sent to communicate the Word of the Lord to lost men."

She nodded. "You mean the church should look outward to its world, not inward to itself?"

"Exactly," I told her. "Also, the church must change its attitude about the world. It must see the community around it as a people in trouble, searching for meaning in a very confusing world. Once the church looks on itself as a lifeboat in a sea of drowning people, it will have no difficulty in accepting its mission of salvation to the lost."

The man who spoke of the moths asked, "But what if they don't want to be saved? What you say would be easy if everybody knew he was drowning. But folks in this town just laugh at you when you tell them they're lost. You know the old saying—you can lead a horse to water, but you can't make him drink."

Now we had gone from moths to horses, and I was not prepared with a horse illustration on church growth. I said, "Of course, everyone won't say yes. The job of the church isn't to convert everyone, but to tell everyone. Each man, woman, and child of our generation must hear a good explanation of the gospel and have a fair chance to accept Christ. But let's not forget that many people don't come to Christ because they don't like what they see in the church. Jesus said His church would be persecuted for its faith . . . but the kind of faith we have most of the time doesn't even catch the world's attention, far less its wrath."

A flurry of approving *amens* told me I was getting through to them. It also told me what kind of church this was.

"What this church needs," I said, "is a good, old-fashioned Jericho march!"

My librarian friend was surprised at me, but the moth man broke into a grin. In religion it is very hard to please literary and country people at the same time. Most of us in that Sunday school class could remember the Jericho marches, when at a high point in the service the people would all march around the inside of the church, singing and shouting and praising God. Today, the practice is often recalled with tones of ridicule, but for those who participated sincerely it was a significant and often spiritual experience. It was not traditional with any of the old-line churches, but it did have a certain biblical precedent. The short-lived practice was at its best when it was spontaneous, and perhaps at its worst when it was contrived. As with many folk practices in religion, it could not survive duplication outside its original setting. It belonged to another time and place, when worshipers were more participants than spectators.

I said, "No, I don't mean what you think. What this church needs is not a Jericho march around the inside of the church, but a real Jericho march around the outside until these walls fall down. We must get outside these four walls and evangelize the real world out in the community."

I went on to tell them that for a church to grow it must take on some of the attitudes of the Children of Israel when they marched around Jericho about 1400 B.C.

First, the Children of Israel obeyed God, even though they did not fully understand all the significance of their assignment. They were to march around the walled city of Jericho once each day for six days, and on the seventh day they were to circle the city seven times. On the last time around, when the priests blew the trumpets, they were to shout. All in all, it was a rather unorthodox battle plan; yet it brought complete victory when the walls of the city fell down.

Archeologists differ on their interpretations of the ruins of old Jericho, but there is general agreement that the city was destroyed about the time of the Israelite invasion. The walls were toppled as if by an earthquake, and the city was burned.

A church may not fully understand how it can totally evangelize a community, but it must first go forth to battle in obedience to God. The assignment of the church to go into all the world and preach the gospel to every creature is clear, even if the immediate methods are difficult to understand. However, although the present assignment may be in question, the outcome is already determined. "This gospel of the kingdom shall be preached" (Matt. 24:14). The command of Joshua is still applicable to our communities today, for he said, "Shout; for the Lord hath given you the city" (Josh. 6:16).

The second attitude we should learn from the original Jericho march is that the Israelites were planning the total conquest of the city. They were not to be satisfied with a conditional compromise with Jericho, nor with establishing only a token presence of Jewish culture within the city; but would settle for nothing less than complete victory.

This same attitude must characterize a congregation if

it is to grow significantly in a community. It must see itself as a center from which the entire community is influenced for Christ. This total community concept is essential to the meaningful growth of a church. It must attempt to reach every person with its message and pervade every facet of community life with its influence.

Yet a third attitude to be learned from Jericho is the importance of public relations. Israel had a public image that struck terror into the hearts of the people of Jericho. The rumors had already reached Jericho that the Red Sea had opened for these people, that their God had spoken to them out of Mount Sinai, and that no armies could resist them. When Israel attacked Jericho by the unorthodox manner of marching around the city and blowing on their rams' horns, the battle was practically won from the first day. Israel had the attitude and the public image of a winner; and Jericho knew from the moment it heard those rams' horns that all was lost.

The church, too, must have a winning attitude. When a football coach was interviewed after the victory of his team, he said, "Winning is a habit, just like losing." Before anything can be accomplished, an idea must first be conceived in the mind and followed by a firm belief that it will succeed. Without such confidence, a church cannot grow significantly.

A congregation must develop a public image and a self-image that it is a successful, growing church where men may find the love of God, the compassion of men, and a purposeful meaning to life. The word must get out that the people of a church know God and are capable of introducing Him to others.

I must remember to tell that Chicago pastor that idealism is not just a luxury. It is absolutely essential to church growth. The Jerichos have always been conquered by the unorthodox dreamers who have dared to break with tradition and believe God for the miracle of definitive success.

4
Giants in the Land

Most active laymen and their pastors have as many church-growth books on their shelves as housewives have cookbooks. Yet, the recipes seldom make the trip from the page to the pulpit and pew. Dinner usually turns out to be the same old meat and potatoes. Exotic recipes for church growth abound, but they always seem to start out with something you don't have.

I went to my wife's rack of cookbooks, selected a random volume with a meat picture on it, and looked up a recipe for roast turkey. Sure enough, the recipe began, "Stuff and truss bird just before roasting." It was a terrific recipe, but it only assumed that I was standing there with bird in hand.

In my opinion, most studies on church growth are much too theoretical. They assume too much. Perhaps it is because most such studies are made by college professors and their students rather than by the practical workers in the field who must actually produce church growth. Much of the available literature on the subject skips the most important part of the church-growth dilemma—the ingredients.

My problem with the turkey recipe was not how to stuff and truss the bird, but where to get one. No amount of study on the subject could produce on my table the condition of roast turkey as long as I had only a hypothetical recipe. Most pastors and laymen know what to do with a church once it starts to grow. Theoretically, they even know how to initiate an expansion pattern. However, in spite of their knowledge, the church still does not grow because some of the main ingredients are missing.

Most of us know what to do with a turkey that is already roasted and served on a platter. Many of us know how to initiate the condition of roast turkey from the time we pick out a frozen bird in the supermarket. Fewer know how to catch a live turkey and dress it for roasting. Even fewer know how to raise a turkey from an egg, feed it, and prepare it for market. The farther back you go in the process, the fewer the people who understand what to do.

Similarly, the basic deterrents to church growth are not to be found in the ignorance of what to do with a church that is growing or about to grow, but in how to motivate a church that seems to lack the fundamental components. The situation is similar to that of the man who said, "If we had some ham, we'd have ham and eggs . . . if we had some eggs."

To continue my turkey story, I asked myself, "What is stopping me from roasting a turkey?" The answer was simple: In my entire supply of foodstuffs there was not one solitary bird. There was neither turkey nor reasonable substitute.

So I further asked myself, "What is stopping me from getting a turkey?" This one was a little harder because it did not deal with a physical fact such as to have or not to have the proper makings for roast turkey. This question probed deeper into my motivation and available resources. Was I sufficiently hungry to spend my hard-earned cash on a dead bird?

I decided to settle for the ingredients at hand and ate a peanut butter-and-honey sandwich. The cookbook was wonderful, but I lacked the motivation, the current resources, and ultimately the ingredients to translate its pages into reality. Many churches do not grow for some of these same reasons. They cannot identify with the church-growth studies because they feel that they don't have the ingredients, they lack the motivation, and they are not willing to pay the price. Consequently, they settle for something far short of what they could become. They are not helped by church-growth books because their real problems are earlier in the sequence than most church-growth studies have gone.

The question we should ask of a church is not, "How can we make this church grow?" but rather, "What is stopping this church from growing?"

Here we must assume that growth is a natural tendency. Even though something similar to growth may appear in a laboratory experiment, real growth only occurs as a result of the spontaneous multiplication of living cells brought about by genetic forces. We cannot cause growth; we can only create the favorable conditions in which growth may occur.

If there is any life at all in a church, we should expect the natural processes of life to produce growth. If the church does not grow, we must examine it for deficiencies and restore to it the proper components of life. To solve the problem, we must not view the failure to grow as a normal pattern of church development, but rather as a serious abnormality. The absence of church growth is a deadly disease for which we must discover the cause and the cure.

We are on the right course, then, when we ask the question: What is stopping this church from growing?

If there is a rock wedged against the front tire of an automobile, no amount of examination of the rest of the car will solve the problem. Even with long discussions about the relative merits of the internal combustion engine, alternative designs for the chassis, or the choice of automatic or manual transmissions, the vehicle will not budge one inch until the driver gives serious consideration to whatever is stopping the car from moving forward.

At this point we are in danger of oversimplifying the issue, for there are many things that can stop the natural development of a church. If we find a dead plant and ask why it is not growing, it is not sufficient to say, "Because it is dead." No amount of *post mortem* examination will restore a dead plant to life.

If a church has any life to it at all, it can be helped; but if it is so bound to tradition that it will not consider alternative methods, it is too far gone for resusitation. There are very few churches that could not be restored to life if they would be willing to sink their roots back into their apostolic origins and participate once more in the doctrines, religious experiences, practices, and priorities of New Testament Christianity. Some churches are more in need of resurrection than restoration, but even the deadest of churches could make the necessary decisions and return to vital Christianity.

There also are situations that make the immediate revitalization of a church unlikely. The list would be very long if we would include all the possibilities, such as the pastor running off with the church secretary, the principal employers in town going out of business, or a new freeway cutting off access to the church parking lot. The beautiful garden of prayer is not always a bed of roses. To cope with such devastating problems, we would have to study each case individually.

In spite of examples of the unconscious and the dead, I still hold to my beliefs that any church can grow if it will create the conditions in which growth occurs, and that we can best determine whether proper conditions exist by asking what stops church growth.

I further believe that the total evangelization of every community on earth must be accomplished by apostolically and task-oriented churches. The great religious need of our world is for a great number of churches to return to the principles of original Christianity and take up once more the apostolic sword of total world evangelization. I also think there are thousands of churches with good pastors and cooperative laymen who are ready and waiting for a call to action. In the first four chapters of this book, we have been looking at the important factors of motivation, attitude, and urgency for church growth. Now let us examine specific problems and recommendations.

When the Children of Israel marched out of Egypt and first approached the Promised Land, they camped at Kadesh-barnea and sent twelve spies into Canaan. The spies came back with the thrilling report that Canaan was a land flowing with milk and honey. All but two, however, reported that Israel could not conquer Canaan because there were giants in the land. As a result, the Children of Israel were stopped from their conquest of Canaan and did not gather the courage to launch another major attack until a new generation of warriors arose thirty-eight years later. Until then, they wandered aimlessly in the Wilderness.

The fact was that their fears were unfounded. The giants were the Anakim, a group of three tribes of exceptionally tall people who lived in southern Canaan around Hebron. The spies said that next to the Anakim the Hebrews were like grasshoppers. Poor defeated people! It took them a generation to forget that they had been slaves. As it turned out, the giants were not even a warlike people. Caleb later claimed that territory for the inheritance of his family and conquered the Anakim without difficulty.

Every church comes to its Kadesh—that decisive moment when it must either go forward or step back. There are minor decisions that bring small victories or temporary setbacks; but also there are major turning points in the life of a church when a set of decisions determines rather permanently the personality and ultimate effectiveness of a congregation. In most cases, a church that pulls back from significant challenges will retreat into a wilderness wandering until its pastor and lay leaders are replaced by a new generation.

In a southern town there was a small church that had occupied an old, back-street building for many years. A young pastor came who found a choice piece of property in a growing section of the town. He studied the church finances and showed the members how they could purchase the land, construct a new building, and move into a new period of development. They held a business meeting, and the congregation voted down the dreams of their young pastor. Within a year the pastor had gone to follow his dreams elsewhere, and the church lost many of its members to a new church in town. Kadesh had struck again!

Is it possible to recognize a place of growth-determining decision when we reach it? Yes, I think it is possible. Of course, it would be a lot easier if there were road signs that said: KADESH—BEWARE OF GIANTS! Unfortunately, the many churches who have visited the location have failed to leave behind them such a convenient reminder of their moments of misjudgment.

The Hebrews knew they were at Kadesh when they asked the question: What will stop us from conquering Canaan? The answer was: We have stopped at Kadesh because there are giants in the land. It was a simple miscalculation based on fear of taking the next giant step forward. So, instead, their next step was backward . . . and it took them a generation to recover from their failure to act decisively in the face of a barrier to their progress.

It is easier to know when you have just been to Kadesh than it is to recognize when you are there, just as the flashing red light of a police car may inform you that you have just run a stop sign. Charlie said, "My house is the one just before you get to the cliff." That's mighty nice of old Charlie, because if you go over the cliff you can say, "Hey, that was Charlie's house back there." Kadesh is like that; you may not know when you are there, but you will always know when you have been there.

You know your church has been to Kadesh when less than one-third of the congregation attends the Sunday night service. You have been to Kadesh when the ladies' aid announces an evangelistic meeting, and it turns out to be a garage sale. You know you've been thére when just before the church team begins a basketball game and you suggest a word of prayer, somebody on the team asks, "Are we really that bad, Coach?" Yes, it's Kadesh when someone toward the back of the sanctuary says, "Praise the Lord," and the whole congregation turns around to see who did it. You've been there when a six-year-old turns to his father in the middle of the pastor's sermon and asks, "Is he live or on tape?" It's Kadesh again when the pastor tells you, "We're not working for numbers, but a deeper life in the Spirit." You know you've been there when the congregation begins to leave the front pews empty, and even the hard-of-hearing don't plug their earphones into the second row.

Most of all, you know your church has backed away from Kadesh when your congregation ceases to grow. When Israel made its strategic error, it stopped conquering new territory; and when a church makes a similar mistake, it stops significant convert-making. And, as in the case of Israel, the trend cannot be reversed until a new generation comes into leadership.

Many decisions are irreversible. Opportunities once shunned seldom return for a second attempt, and choices once made supply the fabric out of which other subsequent choices are made. You can never go back and repair wrong decisions; but with courage and understanding you can make new choices and reverse the trend.

It is difficult to know when it happens, but some factor or combination of factors slows down the progress of a church and grinds it to a tragic halt. The number of believers fluctuates for a while, drops back, tries to increase again, and finally declines. Discouragement sets in, followed by its aftermath of lethargy. New people visit the church, but they do not stay. High school graduates go off to college, and no new young people replace them. The members still like their church, but they regard it with the same feeling of sadness they might experience toward the noticeable decline of a beloved grandmother.

What went wrong? The congregation came to Kadesh, failed to conquer its giants, and retreated to the Wilderness. It is very sad, but it also is a very common ailment among American churches.

Take a careful look at your attendance record. In most churches the only available statistics are those of the Sunday school, so generally we must use them instead of a count of the number of people in the morning worship services. How old is your church? How long has the average attendance remained at its present figure? Is the tendency upward, downward, or fluctuating about a central number? How long has the present trend continued?

I can hear the objections already, saying, "But you can't apply such statistics to religion."

And to that I reply, "Who said so?" On the Day of Pentecost, the apostles knew they had 120 present when the first Christians were baptized in the Holy Spirit. On that same day, "there were added unto them about three thousand souls" (Acts 2:41). The Christian religion started out counting its growing numbers. Whatever happened to change that practice?

Someone has pointed out that the only people in favor of birth control are those who already have been born. Somewhat similarly, the only churches opposed to statistical analysis appear to be those with the poorest examples of statistics to analyze.

While you are examining your attendance records, ask yourself the important question: What is our doubling time? By doubling time, I mean how long it takes your church- to double the size of its congregation. Go back in your attendance records and find out when your Sunday school was half its present size. Was it five years ago? If so, then your church has a present doubling time of five years. If it was 25 years, then that is your doubling time. Now study the records even farther back and see when it was half that size (or a quarter of its present size). Was the second doubling time the same as the first? If not, is your church doubling its size faster or slower than previously? If the present trend continues, how long will it take to double your size again in the future? Will it ever double again?

Let us look at an example—Eastside Assembly of God in Tucson, Arizona, where the pastor is Robert A. Sites. In a report to the congregation, Pastor Sites gave the following annual Sunday school averages:

1962	68	1969	100
1963	78	1970	124
1964	110	1971	191
1965	117	1972	204
1966	124	1973	229
1967	106	1974	272
1968	115	1975	315

The church has doubled in the past five years. Before that, it doubled in eight years. This means that its rate of growth has increased dramatically. If the congregation continues to double every five years, it will have 630 in 1980, 1,260 in 1985, and 2,520 in 1990. As we will consider later, it is now growing through some of its easier stages, so it may slow down for a while around the figures of 400 and 600. It will accomplish a miracle if it grows past 1,200.

Notice that the church had trouble getting past the middle 120s. After an excellent increase from 78 to 110 in 1964, it grew to 124 over the following two years. Then, it dropped back in 1967 and did not reach 124 again until

1970. When it finally passed the 120s in 1971, it shot on up to much higher figures. It shows no signs of slowing down now, but it probably will have to make some changes to accommodate more people in the middle 300s.

Another church with an excellent record of growth is Evergreen Christian Center in Olympia, Washington, where Glen D. Cole is the pastor. This church reports the following statistics:

1964	278	1970	428
1965	257	1971	469
1966	236	1972	612
1967	258	1973	768
1968	321	1974	1,118
1969	382	1975	1,175

This church had some trouble getting out of the middle 200s, but once it broke out of its rut it grew phenomenally. It has a present doubling time of less than three years, after a previous doubling time of four years. It not only is growing in numbers, but its rate of growth is increasing.

If some of my theories are true, it will slow down a bit just under 1,200 while it reorganizes for its next period of growth. I must point out, however, that it already has broken several of my rules for church growth by failing to slow down at my predicted levels at 400, 600, and 800. Apparently, the reason was that when it reorganized for growth, it skipped some of the organizational steps that churches normally develop.

In my own experience as a pastor, I saw my churches grow from 35 to 85 in 18 months with a doubling time of less than one year; from 200 to 318 in six months, which would have arrived at a one-year doubling time if I had not been an interim pastor trying to get to the mission field; and from 400 to 1,000 in two years, with a doubling time of about 18 months. I am currently the promotions director for a worldwide foreign missions program that has doubled its number of members and adherents in the past 6 years, tripled in 12 years, and quadrupled in 16 years, while numbering in the millions.

My own brother, Dan Womack, had a similar experience as pastor of Christian Life Center in Port Orchard, Washington. His church grew from 85 to 212 in two and a half years, with a doubling time of 24 months.

The idea of measuring the doubling time of a church's growth is a very important concept, because a church either must grow or fail in its divine assignment to make converts. If a church grows by 7 percent per year, it will double in 10 years. If it can maintain its 7 percent annual increase, it will double again in the next 10 years. Thus, you may say it has a 7 percent annual growth rate, or a doubling time of 10 years. For example, a church with an attendance of 50 would reach 100 in 10 years and 200 in 20 years. Such growth is much too slow to make any significant religious change in the community.

A healthy, growing church should maintain a long-term doubling time of 4 to 6 years, with occasional thrusts of 2 to 4 years. Thus, a church of 50 might grow to 100 in 6 years, 200 in 10 years, 400 in 16 years, and 800 in 20 years. Even this rate of increase is too slow to accomplish the real task of the church in the world. It is a minimal growth rate to be considered successful at all.

Many churches will catch a vision of greatness and grow much faster than a doubling time of 4 to 6 years. However, most churches will not exceed this rate because of the maturation drag of developing leaders fast enough to keep up with the rapid expansion of the congregation.

Church attendance is torn between two prevailing forces —the tendency toward progress and the tendency toward stasis. The word *stasis* usually refers to an abnormal stoppage of blood in its forward motion through the small vessels and capillaries, or the retarded movement of intestinal contents because of some obstruction or muscular malfunction; but I use the word in this context to mean any stoppage or retardation of a normal process. The static condition of many churches results from the stasis in their programs.

It is as though the winds were blowing in one direction while the ocean currents were flowing in another; and the church, like some weathered old ship, sails courageously at the heart of the resulting storm. The church lives and moves at the dynamic point of convergence of these two forces, and the prevalence of one over the other determines the forward or backward movement of the congregation. Thus, the church is always in a storm of conflict between its own inclinations to incite change or to establish stability. The pastor and lay leaders, like wise seamen, must sail their ship with a dauntless will to make progress while still showing great respect for the congregation's inclination to maintain stability.

It seems to me that the comparison of the church to a vessel floating in a stormy sea is a true picture of the church's condition in the world. Christ's illustration of the church upon a rock is excellent for its description of the sure foundation of the people of God; but it does not speak to the constantly changing condition of church growth. Apostolic Christian doctrine is solid as a rock; but church attendance is as fluid and as unpredictable as the sea, and many a congregation lies shipwrecked on the shore for failing to recognize the necessity of proper navigation.

The tendencies toward progress and stasis are always present as though they were two arrows pointing in opposite directions. The position of the church is at the center at the very point of impact between them. Sometimes the arrows point inward, forcing the church to overorganize its structure, attempting to grow while still yielding to the temptation to establish apparent order out of apparent chaos. At other times, the arrows point outward, tearing the church apart from its stability and allowing its interests to wander over a wide field of fruitless possibilities.

The natural inclination of the church is to spread to a widening circle of people who have been influenced in some favorable way. Each person who is helped by the church will pass the good news along to other people with whom he comes in contact. As you multiply the number of people in the congregation, you theoretically increase your potential points of contact with the community and hence should increase your rate of growth as the church expands.

However, there is the second tendency at work to slow down anything that is growing and bring it into balance with the rest of the system. This is true in biology where life forms fill all the available environmental niches and then compete with one form against another to maintain an ecological balance. It also happens in sociology, where the wont toward stasis reveals itself as that principle of human life that seeks social stability and fears unpredictable change. We may find another comparison in physics, for this resistance to progress is similar to the influence of inertia on the forward momentum on a moving object.

The problem is surprisingly complex, for a church must somehow yield to both tendencies at the same time. A church must have both growth and stability. Unmanaged growth can result in a disordered mass of people who lack the Christian virtues and serve no godly or earthly purpose; while nongrowing stability can solidify into an inflexible monument to past accomplishment.

When I was a boy, we found some seeds in an unmarked envelope, so we planted them to see what would come up. This was no Jack-and-the-Beanstalk story, for the seeds grew into a mass of leafy vegetation that developed no noticeable flowers for decoration, produced no fruit for eating, was not itself edible as a vegetable, and did not grow tall enough for shade. The seeds grew all right, but none of us ever knew what they turned out to be. Growth for its own sake can produce congregations much like my unidentified garden phenomenon.

The rocks in my garden were very stable. I did not have to concern myself about their growth, for they had not changed considerably in millions of years. Stability without change is deadly.

The successfully growing church must maintain a steady pattern of expansion with a meaningful doubling time of six years or less, while still maintaining a dynamic stability that develops with the changing needs of the congregation. This means that as a church grows it must continuously reappraise its organization and its methods of administration to keep pace with the numerical expansion.

The goal of a congregation must be to grow and maintain organizational stability at the same time. The natural tendency of a moderately growing church is to work in cycles rather than developing a steady program of organized growth. The result is that a church will grow for a while, and then it will slow down to readjust its organization to the new size of the congregation. If it reorganizes correctly, it will begin to grow again, after which it will once more slow down to allow its structure to readjust to the new conditions. The problem is that each time the church restructures, it hardens the mold a little more and makes future changes more difficult. There are longer and longer gaps between the growth periods as the structure becomes less adaptable, and finally the cycles of growth cease altogether.

It is easy to say that the church must grow and adapt its structure at the same time, but the two activities seldom operate simultaneously in such an ideal balance. For a church to grow continuously, the pastor and his leading laymen must be aware of the two tendencies and must give to both of them their equal attention. As the church becomes larger, the congregation can carry on its activities at many different levels and go through its normal cycles of growing and restructuring on a departmental level with only occasional major adjustments.

The situation is like the problem of inflating a balloon. With each puff of air into the balloon the rubber must adjust itself to the new quantity of gasses within its expanding periphery. The expansion and the adaptation to accommodate growth must both happen at the same time. As the balloon is filled to capacity, the structure becomes less and less adaptable to further expansion. At last, it reaches the critical point when it must cease to grow or explode. As a church grows it must adjust its organization to accommodate its new members and adherents. The tragedy of the exploding balloon seldom happens to churches because most churches cease to expand long before their structure collapses.

Change itself is a frightening thought. It is not that men do not think creatively; it is rather that they reject such a thought out of fear of the unknown—the insecurity of new factors they might not be able to control. So, they construct a safe set of concepts with a predictable group of people responding in a predetermined way. The resulting condition is unreal because it is contrived. It is ineffective because it is out of touch with reality. The actors in this drama touch each other only at the points of their assent, never talking about the vast world that lies behind that false backdrop of their make-believe stage.

We recognize, then, that one of the major forces that stops church growth is the failure to adapt the organization of the church to the condition of congregational expansion. As the structure of the church becomes more and more fixed, the continued growth of the congregation becomes increasingly unlikely.

Yet another factor that stops church growth is a low level of congregational intensity. Strong effects must be accompanied by strong feelings on the part of the participants. It takes more than muscle, bone, and brain to produce a winning athlete; it also requires some strong spurts of adrenalin into the system. A church does not need to be keyed up to a feverish pitch all the time, but if it wants to grow it must be enthusiastic.

John Wesley, in a sermon on "The Nature of Enthusiasm," said, "There is no man excellent in his profession, whatsoever it be, who has not in his temper a strong tincture of enthusiasm."

I once pastored a church where the head deacon fell asleep in every service. On my first couple of Sundays in the little church he managed to stay awake with the helpful assistance of his wife's elbow; but once he decided that my doctrine was all right, he eased back into his weekly habit. He claimed that religion was very relaxing for his nervous condition. Fortunately, the rest of the congregation did not require the power of God to perform such a miracle of relaxation, and the church doubled its number in eighteen months.

Lord Byron wrote of boredom as, "That awful Yawn which Sleep cannot abate." Boredom is contagious. Have you ever noticed what happens when one person yawns in public? It triggers the same response in other people. Once the pastor's voice becomes a monotonous drone and a few people fall asleep on the front pew, you may as well pronounce the benediction.

If a church gets in a habitual rut and becomes predictable, boredom is inevitable. It hardly seems possible that anyone could become bored with the presence of God, but perhaps the very key to church boredom is that the people do not sense His presence in a dull service where the pastor is uninspired and the congregation is half asleep.

The prevailing emotion of a congregation should be one of enthusiasm. Bulwer-Lytton said, "Nothing is so contagious as enthusiasm; it moves stones, it charms brutes. Enthusiasm is the genius of sincerity, and truth accomplishes no victories without it."

Much of the condition of a church can be measured by its degree of enthusiasm. If people sincerely believe in their church, their favorable feelings will be evident in their whole attitude toward the church. This enthusiasm will show itself not only in the emotional tone of the services, but also in the friendliness of the people. The Book of Proverbs declares, "A man that hath friends must shew himself friendly" (Prov. 18:24). So a church that attracts new friends must demonstrate a sincere and friendly enthusiasm.

Another limitation to church growth is the separation of a church from its apostolic origins. It is possible, of course, for even a non-Christian religious group to grow. However, true Christian growth results from true Christian seed, found only in the original substance of apostolic doctrine, religious experiences, practices, and priorities.

There is an important passage in the Epistle to the Hebrews, which says, "Let us lay aside every weight, and the sin which doth so easily beset us, and let us run with patience the race that is set before us, looking unto Jesus the author and finisher of our faith" (Heb. 12:1-2).

It is uncertain which of the first-century writers composed this masterpiece. The Epistle to the Hebrews shows the influence of the apostle Paul, but the Greek language is not in his style. The closest New Testament style to that of Hebrews is the writing of Luke, who wrote both the Gospel of Luke and the Book of Acts; but the book was probably written by one of the other associates of Paul, such as Epaphroditus.

The passage tells us that the church should be task-oriented, dedicated to "run with patience the race that is set before us." The task of the church is to worship God, preserve and teach true Christian doctrine, provide fellowship for the believers, and evangelize the world. By characterizing the task as a race, the writer warns us of its urgency and tells us that we must have a winning attitude about it. We know we must hurry, but we also know we must win. To this sense of confident urgency we may apply the words of Jesus, "I must work the works of him that sent me, while it is day: the night cometh, when no man can work" (John 9:4).

To run this race, we must "lay aside every weight, and the sin which doth so easily beset us."

The weights we must lay aside are the external accumulations of non-Christian influences and practices. We must lay aside all external traditions not learned from apostolic Christianity, for all such unnecessary baggage weighs down the church and eventually stops its forward progress.

Jude says, "Ye should earnestly contend for the faith which was once delivered unto the saints" (Jude 3). John said, "This is the commandment, That, as ye have heard from the beginning, ye should walk in it" (2 John 6). Paul warned, "But though we, or an angel from heaven, preach any other gospel unto you than that which we have preached unto you, let him be accursed" (Gal. 1:8).

There is little question that the apostles intended that the Christian religion would always teach the doctrines, religious experiences, practices, and priorities of that "faith that was once delivered unto the saints." That original faith is the apostolic seed that will grow once again if we give it the chance.

There once was a packet of apostolic seed that was spilled on the soil of the ancient Roman Empire and commissioned to become the dominant life form on the whole earth. When the seeds began to grow and take root, they multiplied rapidly. As their fruit was recognized by their enemies they were persecuted bitterly; but the opposition only served to scatter the seeds far and wide.

When opposition failed to stop that original life, other plants attempted to blend with the seed to form hybrid varieties that would be less dominating, less apt to choke out the other existing plants. For a while, the hybrid experiment appeared to work, for the apostolic plant was crossbred with strange plants until only vestiges of the original plant remained.

Just when the plant seemed well under control, somebody discovered some original seed tucked away in a forgotten book and sowed it once more across northern Europe. The reaction was violent, but the true plant began to grow again. Its purity dominated over the weaker hybrid varieties, and once more it threatened to spread across the earth.

Having failed to stop it by opposition and crossbreeding, the enemy tried a third method of attack. He would allow the seeds to grow, but would capture them in controlled beds, safely guarded in special hothouses designed to limit their growth to manageable proportions. Their sunlight would come through stained-glass windows, and the world outside would never know of their marvelous life.

That is the condition today. The original seed is pure, and its nature is unmixed with hybrid varieties; but it no longer exists in a wild state. Protected by its own enemies, who pose as its friendly naturalists, it demonstrates its wonderful foliage and its delicious fruit behind protective glass where it cannot compete in the open environment of the earth. As long as it is so concealed in its domesticated state, it will never fulfill its task of world domination.

What is the answer?

The plant must break out of its stained-glass sanctuary and take its life into the open fields. Its seeds must be scattered on the soil of every nation. It must be nurtured, encouraged, turned loose in its wild, uncontrollable state. It must be freed to the force of the wind and the driving of the rain, for the seed carries in its cells the knowledge of its own destiny. It must take root and bear fruit in every conceivable environment on the face of the planet, and when it does so this age will come to an end.

Yes, the church must lay aside every weight of its unfortunate hybridization with the other religious life of the world. It also must lay aside its own internal sins, those weaknesses of human nature that slow it down from running its race. It must defy its own weaknesses of lethargy, lack of momentum, lack of intensity, lack of enthusiam. Dwight L. Moody said, "The world has yet to see what God will do with and for and through and in and by the man who is fully and wholly consecrated to Him. . . . I will try my utmost to be that man."

If we are to run this race with patience, then we must lay aside every external tradition and every internal weakness that will slow down our progress or deter us from fulfilling our divine assignment.

To accomplish our task, we must keep "looking unto Jesus the author and finisher of our faith." Jesus Christ is the ultimate object of our faith. Our whole goal is to love and praise Him, to do what He told us to do in this world, and to be with Him forever in heaven.

I have translated this passage from the Greek text: "Having laid aside every impediment and the sin that so easily walls us in, with determination we should run the race lying before us, keeping our eyes on Jesus, the one who begins our faith and brings it to a successful completion."

As the author and finisher of our faith, Jesus assures us of His presence and help from the beginning of our race to the end. As we begin the race, He is there to fire the starting gun; and when we come to the finish line, He will be there to give us the checkered flag.

In another passage, the Lord tells us, "I am Alpha and Omega, the beginning and the ending, saith the Lord, which is, and which was, and which is to come, the Almighty" (Rev. 1:8).

He who started us in our divine task intends also for us to finish it. He is our source of authority, of power, of creativity, and of ability to bring to completion the work He has begun in us.

Of course, there are giants in the land! Are we to dedicate our lives to a cause without challenges? The greater the obstacles, the sweeter will be our ultimate victory.

The Lord never said it would be easy to evangelize the

world. He just commanded us to do it, and He promised us His continued presence until the end of the age.

5

The Pyramid Builders

We now come to the most difficult and what I consider to be the most important single factor in producing church growth. In the previous chapter, I told you that a church will grow by its own tendency toward social expansion if we discover what stops it from growing and remove such obstacles from the church's path. What I said is true, but it is only a partial solution to the problem. In addition to the removal of obstacles—those giants in the land—we must create the conditions in which growth will occur.

Natural growth is always preceded by a creative act, and the nature of the developing life form that results will carry with it the characteristics of its originating parents. Not every stroke of genius will cause satisfactory church growth, any more than the procreative act of any two random examples of life will produce a desirable result. Joke-telling sessions abound with stories of crossing two unlikely parents to produce some absurd offspring. (What do you get if you cross an elephant and a parrot? A beast that not only remembers, but talks about it!) It is not enough that a congregation be creative to produce growth; it must create the right conditions in which growth may occur.

Creativity itself is such an elusive thing that few people ever capture it and put it to domesticated use. It seems as though the agent that can cause growth is harder to recognize and use than the very condition of growth that we are trying to attain. In this field, however, the Christian has an advantage over thinkers in other professions. The notion of creativity is very much related to the idea of spirit—a subject for which the church claims considerable knowledge and experience.

Creativity is so integrally a part of the nature of God that no individual believer, pastor, or church can truly comprehend or worship Him without at one and the same time being creative in spirit and innovative in action.

What is creativity? Most people know it has something to do with imagination, intuition, and just plain guesswork. Some writers have it part of the time. So do some artists, some musicians, and some scientists. The fact is that nobody really knows what it is or how it works; but we can sometimes identify its footprints and tell where it has been. Creativity will at times appear to make something out of nothing, as in the case of God's creation of the world; and at other times it will produce some result out of an apparently unrelated source, as when Jesus turned the water into wine at the marriage in Cana. Whenever mere men display creative ability, they are apt to claim divine inspiration; and the men who observe the application of creativity are apt to call the result ingenious.

Actually, creativity is probably much more common among all men than is often supposed. It is basically the power of the mind to synthesize ideas from two or more previously unconnected ideas. Writers, artists, musicians, and scientists only appear to be more creative than the average man because they constantly feed random information into their minds as purposeful fuel for creative combustion. They are people of imagination and intuition because they are inquisitive about everything about them. Creativity only comes to those who ask questions, who seek solutions to problems.

Many people are afraid to allow themselves to think creatively. They look on an unsolved problem as a threatening monster seeking to devour them, rather than as an opportunity for new experience and possible progress. The creative mind always reaches out for new alternatives. It engages in what some writers have called possibility thinking. Instead of saying, "This is the way we've always done it," it asks, "What if we would try doing it this way?" In fact, the what-if approach to a subject is at the very heart of the creative process.

At some uncountable time in the very distant past, God must have said, "What if I were to make a funny little world with a lot of strange creatures on it? What if I would place that world so far from my other islands of life in the universe that it could not upset the rest of my creation? And then, what if I would give one of those creatures the gift of intelligence so he could be more like Me? What if he would begin to make his own decisions and would turn against Me?" God's thoughts went infinitely beyond this description, but at least the what-if characteristic must have been involved in His decision to do what He did on this lonely little planet.

People fear creativity because to them it represents disorder. Creativity changes everything it touches. When I was entering the ministry, my father told me, "Son, never leave anything the way you find it." It was a rather sweeping directive, but my life has been so involved in introducing changes to people's lives that I often remember his words.

In a book called *The Creative Process*, Brewster Ghiselin said, "One might suppose it easy to detect creative talent and to recognize creative impulse and creative work. But the difficulties are considerable. Because every creative act overpasses the established order in some way and in some degree, it is likely at first to appear eccentric to most men." (A Mentor Book, published by The New American Library, New York, 1952, p. 13.)

Writing in the field of scientific creativity, Albert Rosenfeld said, "It is clear that discovery and invention in both science and art require the exercise of creative imagination. And the creative process seems to be basically the same in both fields: a mind trained and attuned to possibilities, an immense amount of work and methodical planning, then leaps of intuitive insight followed by swift consolidation." (Introduction to "The Scientists" section in *The Creative Experience*, edited by Stanley Rosner and Lawrence E. Abt, A Delta Book, published by Dell Publishing Co., Inc., New York, 1970, p. 6.)

Ghiselin agrees with Rosenfeld, for he said, "Even the most energetic and original mind, in order to reorganize or extend human insight in any valuable way, must have attained more than ordinary mastery of the field in which it is to act, a strong sense of what needs to be done, and skill in the appropriate means of expression." (*Op. cit.*, p. 29.)

What apparently is needed for creativity to occur is a willingness to explore new possible solutions, a thorough study of the subject, and the discipline to capture and define those intuitive leaps of the mind that produce alternative ideas.

Creativity most often happens when a problem-oriented thought, caught roving through a wondering but well-informed mind, collides with an unexpected and apparently unrelated image and merges into a synthesized solution.

It is important to view creativity as the explosive impact of two previously unconnected ideas, resulting in the merging of the two into one solution to a problem. In most cases, one idea will be an abstract thought related to a problem and the other will be a more concrete image. For example, just now I faced the problem of explaining to you how two ideas merge into one solution. My mind reached out for a creative answer to my problem, and it compared this merging of ideas to an explosive impact. By so doing, I was able to show that the two ideas come together, interact, and are changed by the dynamic juncture. My problem thought was abstract, but I combined it with a visual image of an explosion to produce a single effect.

Creativity is not like some ancient Muse that comes or goes of its own will. It is rather the result of the comparison of problem-related thoughts to free-association images within a well-informed and inquisitive mind. The results of such creative thinking are not guaranteed to work successfully. In fact, most creative thoughts go into the wastebasket where they belong. The creative process puts out a great number of rejected solutions. It takes an additional level of creativity and discipline to sort out the products of the mind, compare them to the other elements in the problem, and choose the solution that will indeed solve the problem without being inconsistent with other factors or causing greater difficulties than it might solve.

Man can only achieve what he can conceive. That is, if he cannot think about a thing, he cannot do it. Things can happen to him that he does not understand, but he cannot purposefully make something happen if he does not first conceive it in his mind. For example, he may be struck by a falling meteorite without even knowing what hit him, but to launch himself out into space to pursue the culprit he must visualize a great many concepts and create in his mind a whole set of ideas that embrace most of the combined knowledge of the human race.

Church growth, too, requires creative thinking. It is not something that happens rarely by some divine decree, for God has commanded that all Christians make converts among all nations. Rather, church growth results from the creation of the conditions in which congregational expansion will naturally occur.

To make a church grow, we must first conceive of such growth in our minds. A church with 50 in Sunday school must see itself as destined to reach higher numbers. A church with 230 members must visualize its sanctuary filled with 400 worshipers. A congregation can only achieve what it can conceive. Pastor Glen Cole of Evergreen Christian Center in Olympia, Washington, uses his Easter morning attendance as a model for his church growth over the following year. The people in his church visualize a new congregational size, and for the past several years they have attained and even surpassed their goals.

A church, then, not only grows by the removal of obstacles but by the creation of new self-images. Before a church can move to a new level, the leaders of the church must have in their minds a working model—a creative image about themselves and what they want to attain.

The advanced Indian cultures of the Americas—the Incas, the Chibchas, the Mayas, and the Aztecs—made many outstanding discoveries, but they never invented the wheel. None of them ever thought about a wheel because no one had ever seen a wheel. The simple solution of moving an object by connecting it to a revolving disc with an axle through its center never even entered their minds. They had no large animals for pulling anything, so the subject just never occurred to them.

Until recently, there were very few American churches with more than 1,200 people in active attendance. Such churches still are rare, but their number is increasing. What happened? Did Americans suddenly start liking larger churches? Probably not. Rather, some pastors and their congregations have caught new insight into how to organize and administer a church of over 1,200. Most churches are at the size for which they have conceived their image of church ministry and government.

For a church to grow it must produce a new working model—a new self-image. If it sees itself as a reclusive little group of people who meet to hide away from the outside world, it probably will not grow past a few dozen somewhat paranoid people. It must see itself in a new way if it is to grow. If a church of 150 people sees itself as a secure group of religious people with a congregation large enough to pay its own bills, afford a nice pastor, and take adequate care of its members, it will not grow appreciably.

However, if a congregation sees itself as a body of God's servants with an assignment to worship the Lord, preserve and teach apostolic doctrine and experience, provide fellowship for Christian people, and pervade the community and the world with knowledge of the gospel of Christ, then it must grow or utterly fail in its purpose.

In an article in *Life* magazine (October 27, 1972), Dr. Edwin Land, inventor of the Polaroid Land camera, said, "If you are able to state a problem—any problem—and if it is important enough, then the problem can be solved."

We can state our problem clearly enough:

1. Jesus Christ commanded His church to evangelize the whole earth, but many congregations of believers are not making significant progress toward the fulfillment of this Great Commission;

2. Many congregations do not see themselves in the role of community or world evangelization, hence they do not contribute to the common cause of Christian churches; and,

3. Even in those cases where a congregation recognizes its task and identifies with the cause of total evangelization of its community and its world, it is difficult to achieve the concepts to make a congregation grow significantly.

The solution to this problem is for every congregation to accept the divinely appointed task of the Great Commission as its primary objective, to visualize itself in the role of community and world evangelization, and to seek the concepts that will produce significant growth. Unfortunately, this brings us right back to the principles of growth. If a church accepts the challenge of the Great Commission and views itself as responsible for its fulfillment, then there only remains the necessity of capturing the dynamics of growth itself.

I have said that the church needs a new working model, a new way of thinking about itself, before it can move into a fresh period of growth. A church grows by reaching into the future by faith, creating a new context for its self-image, and then moving decisively into its new conceptual environment and claiming the captured territory for its own. Here we come back to the concept that creativity often results from the explosive impact of an abstract idea with a visual image. We want our church to grow, so we envision it as expanding into a new numerical size and appropriate organizational structure. Having created that new format in our minds, we move into our new environment and make ourselves at home in it. When we have outgrown that house, we reach out and create another one in our minds and move into it. We develop a mental image of a new working model and turn that image into a reality; then we repeat the process again and again, each time growing larger in numbers and expanding correspondingly in administrative structure. Each new growth plateau is a step of faith, for faith always reaches into the future. The apostle Paul said, "Now faith is the substance of things hoped for, the evidence of things not seen" (Heb. 11:1).

I discussed this step-of-faith approach with a pastor in Ohio, and he gave it a rather skeptical reception. He said, "This doesn't sound like religion. It's more like what you read in those self-help books. First God created man in His image, and now you're supposed to create yourself in your own image. You're putting too much trust in the mind of the individual. People aren't capable of creating the concepts you're talking about."

I did not argue with him about the comparison between religious and secular self-help books. However, the pastor did raise a problem for my step-of-faith approach to church growth. He was probably right about most people not knowing how to develop some of these concepts for themselves. It is not enough to tell people to think creatively; I must lead the way by providing some new working models for the church.

We are now at a place analagous to my earlier story about the turkey recipe. I have called for the main ingredient of creating a working model of an expanding church, and now I must demonstrate how it is done. That is, I must provide a new paradigm by bringing our growth problem into explosive impact with an adequate visual image.

Once already in this book I have pictured the church as a junk dealer's cart accumulating too many religious relics until it finally collapses under its antiquated load. That could be a working model for some churches, but it is a negative image that leads to decline rather than growth.

In another place I illustrated the proper condition of the church as a lifeboat seeking to save drowning men in a troubled sea. That paradigm told us something about the ministry of the church, but it would make an incomplete working model for other aspects of church life.

In my search for a new working model, I have concluded that in some important ways the church may be compared to a pyramid . . . up to a point, of course!

Really, a pyramid provides a very fitting working model for the church. It is a marvelous invention of man, for it points toward heaven, it can't fall over, and many people believe it possesses mysterious powers. How like the church! Agelessly stable, very impressive, and doing little but reminding us of the glories of the past.

A pyramid meets with the requirement of our working model, for it is one of the oldest visual images of mankind. Its base is a perfect square, and its sides are four perfect isosceles triangles whose base line is slightly longer than its two sides. If you make four such triangles and lean them together so that they form a point at the top and square at the base, you have a pyramid. Utter simplicity, massive size, and remote antiquity combined to make the Egyptian pyramids one of the Seven Wonders of the ancient world.

The Great Pyramid at Gizeh, finished about 2800 B.C., was built of more than two million stone blocks, most of which weighed over two and a half tons. Napoleon Bonaparte claimed there was enough stone in it to build a wall ten feet high and one foot thick all around France. The real purpose of the structure was to build a tomb all around the Pharaoh Khufu (or Cheops). In spite of its massive defenses, tomb robbers apparently broke into it and emptied its burial chambers several thousand years ago.

Some people claim the Great Pyramid was not a tomb at all, but a special chamber for occult meditation. They say that every man is a prisoner within his personal aura— an enveloping energy field that is supposed to resist psychic communication—and that one can escape this aura by being hidden away deeply within solid stone of certain types. Thus, they believe the pyramids were built as psychic chambers for ancient priests to go on long extrasensory journeys of the mind to explore the wonders of the occult world.

Even today, there are those who claim amazing powers for the shape of the pyramid. A Czechoslovakian engineer in Prague is said to have taken out a patent for a pyramid-shaped container that is supposed to keep a razor blade sharp even if its owner shaves with it every day. Pyramid-shaped cartons are supposed to keep milk from going sour. Tents in the form of pyramids are supposed to be marvelous for occult meditation, dynamic ways to sleep, and keeping wild game from spoiling, although not all at the same time. More than one writer probably has considered storing old manuscripts in pyramid boxes.

Astro-archeologist Gerald S. Hawkins has added a new dimension to our understanding of the Gizeh Pyramid by claiming that its sides point to the spot where the sun rises on the first day of spring. In his book *Beyond Stonehenge* (Harper & Row, Publishers, New York: 1973, page 216), he said, "The sides of the Gizeh Pyramids run exactly east-west, azimuth 90°, accurate to the limit of human-eye measurement. How this was done by the builders is not known. It was not done by sighting the pole star, because in 2800 B.C. there was no star visible to the naked eye at or near the celestial pole. No matter how it was done, the sides of the pyramids do point to the sunrise on the first day of spring, the vernal equinox."

Yes, the pyramids do provide a very interesting model for the church. They are memorials to the past, they are thought to possess mysterious powers, and they are celestially oriented. We could find many more similarities if we would let our minds dwell on the subject, not the least of which would be that they are immovable. An atomic explosion would probably do little but glaze their limestone surfaces.

The qualities of a pyramid describe a stable church very well. How then can a pyramid provide a new working model for church growth?

King Khufu faced the same problem nearly 5,000 years ago. He originally ordered his burial chamber to be tunneled into the rock with a moderately humble, medium-sized pyramid to be built on top of it. Time and a growing ego changed his mind, and he ordered the pyramid made larger, even though the construction was nearing completion. The workers labored for years to grant the pharaoh's request. Then (Wouldn't you know it?), the older and then more powerful pharaoh commanded the pyramid to be made even larger! He wanted his burial chamber above the mere earth and located near the very heart of the structure. As a result, there are three separate burial chambers in the Gizeh Pyramid and there is evidence that the size of the structure was increased twice.

I have chosen the pyramid as a working model for a growing church because the same principles involved in making a pyramid larger apply to making a church larger.

To increase the size of their pyramid, the workers at Gizeh had to expand their base in all directions from the original pyramid and then fill in the stone until it completely covered the first stage. Later, when Khufu ordered another enlargement, they repeated the process of expanding the base and filling in the mass. Herein lies the secret of making a pyramid grow: You must expand the base and increase the mass. Base expansion and mass increment are not two separate actions, but must be accomplished simultaneously one in relationship to the other.

The same Pyramid Principle applies to church growth. The mass in this case is the number of people who make up the congregation. To say that the church has grown, has added to its number of adherents, or has increased its mass are the same thing. Our goal is to make the church grow larger, so in effect we must increase the mass to attain this result.

As with the pyramid, however, the church cannot add substantially to its numbers without also expanding its base of operations. In order to care for more people, the church must expand its base of ministry and administration.

There is a dynamic relationship between the size of the congregation and the development of the ministry and administration of a church. Each increase in congregational size demands a corresponding shift in the operational base. Conversely, a premeditated development in the level of ad ministration will often produce subsequent numerical increase. Just as the mass of a pyramid cannot possibly be increased without first expanding the base, so in congregational growth the expansion of ministry and administration occur before added numbers of people begin to attend. Such growth appears to happen in cycles of three actions: expand base, increase mass, stabilize—expand base, increase mass, stabilize.

Growth often appears to happen spontaneously, because the period of increment generally occurs some time after the organizational expansion that caused it. This is one of the reasons why one learns so little by observing growing churches. The time to observe a church is during the period of organizational and administrative changes before the church begins to grow. Unfortunately, these processes are usually done at some subconscious or intuitive level, and a church only later points back to the basal expansion that made possible the subsequent growth.

When we speak of church growth, then, we mean something more than numerical increase. We also mean the expanded development of the ministry and administration of the church to care for a given number of people.

Many churches have failed to grow because they have not understood this simple rule: Organizational expansion always precedes numerical increase. A church may try to grow past its administrative limitations, but it will always drop back to the level of efficiency of the pastor, staff, and lay leaders.

Perhaps we can better understand this principle if we observe another variation of the pyramid working model. Imagine a square table. Now imagine someone pouring sand onto the exact center of the table. As the mass of sand increases, it builds a cone in the middle of the tabletop. When the pile of sand finally grows large enough to reach the edges of the table, it pours off the edges onto the floor. Due to the square shape of the table, we soon have a pyramid of sand that fully covers the table top.

Now a very interesting thing happens. There is no possible way we can increase the size of our tabletop pyramid, because any sand that we add to the pile will just slide down the surface and pour onto the floor. Even a single grain of sand will not remain on the pyramid, for we have reached the ultimate possible growth.

There is only one way we can make our sand pyramid grow; that is to make the table larger. If we build additional leaves onto the table to form a larger base, we can then add to our mass of sand and produce a larger pyramid.

In a similar manner a church cannot grow beyond the dimensions of its base—a combination of ministry and administration. A minister with his staff and lay leaders can care for only a given number of people efficiently. When that efficiency level is reached, the church will cease to grow.

Most American churches tend to level off at predictable numbers of adherents, and the longer they remain at these barrier points the less apt they are ever to surpass them. In most cases, churches make their adjustments to new structure when they make changes in their pastoral staff. A new pastor comes, sets up his form of ministry and administration, and brings the church to a level just short of his peak of efficiency. If the people involved understand this phenomenon, they can seek ways to raise the efficiency level by introducing better organization, more businesslike office procedures, or more staff. Sometimes the need is for more physical space. A major problem is that a pastor and his staff are apt to shift the blame for retarded church growth onto some minor factor or to the congregation itself, rather than accepting the responsibility and making the necessary adjustment in their methods and organization. For this reason, the pastor who starts a church seldom takes it past 90 in attendance, the next pastor probably will not see the average attendance go past 120, and the next will not bring the church farther than 180. More likely, the second pastor will lack the drive of the founder and will drop back to the American average of about 90 in Sunday school, where the church will most probably remain for generations.

If pastors, staff members, and lay leaders could only catch the vision of church growth in cycles of administrative expansion and congregational increase, they could enjoy a steady pattern of continuous growth over a long period of time. It should not be necessary to change pastors to make the church grow; for every congregation and its pastor are potentially capable of raising their level of efficiency, improving their methods of organization, and expanding their ministry to care for more people. There is no logical reason why a group of people and their pastor cannot be honest with themselves and make the necessary adjustments for congregational growth. Most congregations will not make the needed changes without some major revolution in the church, because every day the old system becomes more and more ingrained in their minds and less apt to change. It then becomes impossible to grow without a pastoral change—a religious but not very spiritual gambling game whose odds are as much in favor of church decline as they are for growth. The very purpose of this book is to inspire laymen and their pastors to change their concepts about the church and to move ahead for a new experience of continuous growth in spite of all obstacles and past problems.

Although there are always exceptions to any rule, it is my experience that most churches tend to level off at certain stages of growth. These stages seem to cluster about certain numbers of believers. Such clusters tend to occur around the numbers 50, 90, 120, 180, 230, and 290. A high percentage of American churches cluster about one of these figures. As a church grows larger than the middle 300s, it becomes less predictable, not because there are not similar barriers to growth but because there are fewer examples to establish trends and because they may vary by a wider margin than does a smaller church. The next barriers seem to be just short of 400, 600, 800, and 1,200. Few pastors and their congregations have learned how to organize a church with more than 1,200 to 1,400 in attendance, so there are insufficient samples to establish trend lines beyond that point.

Not all these numerical stages are equally stable. The principal organizational shifts are needed at 50, 90, 120, the mid-200s or early 300s, somewhere around 600, and just short of 1,200. Beyond that, the church ceases to be one congregation, but becomes a conglomerate of many congregations meeting around one central axis. Most congregations would do well to consider dividing into two or more churches at that level of growth.

When a new church is started, it usually grows to 50 with little difficulty. This is because most churches are begun with two or more interested families. Often they are already religious people who have been driving too far to church or are dissatisfied with their present choice of churches. Almost any new congregation can gather 50 people. However, the next 25 are nearly impossible to find. Once the new church has gathered to itself those religious people who are willing to join a new venture, they then must begin to make new converts from among the unchurched of the community. Few nonreligious people are willing to join a small church where they are sure to be asked to lead something, so even those who are converted in the little church will tend to join some other larger congregation. The church stabilizes at 50.

When the church does not continue to grow, the pastor must work at some secular job to support himself and his family (who themselves may make up a tenth of the congregation). The church is closed except for service hours. It is run down because the congregation cannot afford even the pastor's salary, far less any improvements in the property. The pastor has little help, so he does everything himself from preaching to mowing the lawn. In fact, he pays most of the church bills. Eventually, the original pastor leaves, and another man comes who is satisfied to work secularly and pastor a church on the side. The congregation remains at 50 indefinitely. Finally, the few families intermarry until no new person can join the congregation without marrying into the clan. Very often the church will be dominated by an old grandma and her tribe of married sons and daughters. In fact, it is surprising how often such social structures are matriarchal. Once this clan pattern sets in, the church will never develop further, at least for another generation.

If a church can break out of the 50 range and get past about 65 in attendance, it most probably will grow to about

90. Here again it will stabilize. The number 90 is very popular, for many American congregations are clustered about this favorite size. The church building is still closed except for service hours, and if there is a church telephone it rings in the parsonage. The pastor still does almost everything by himself. In this size congregation, many pastors give full time to the church, but their wives work at secular jobs. Some teenager cuts the lawn, and there is a list on the bulletin board of the volunteers who clean the church. The choir makes up for its lack of talent and leadership with its undaunted enthusiasm. There are some good individual Sunday school teachers, but little Sunday school organization. It is very hard for any new leaders to develop among the laymen because the pastor sees them as a threat rather than a blessing.

One of the reasons for the stability of this congregational size is that 90 is about the number of people that one man can pastor without organizing the workers, establishing the discipline of office hours, or planning programs. It is the upper limit of effective pastoring without any planned administrative system.

Another reason for the stability at 90 is related to the clan pattern again. If the church remains at this level for very long, two or three strong family leaders will dominate the church and protect its positions of influence for their clan members. The church is large enough for their purposes, and if a pastor begins to bring in new blood and put nonclan members to work they will rebel and quickly stifle the new growth. Unless they allow the pastor to use new people, the church will remain at 90 or less over a long period, as many churches apparently have done.

Clans will develop in all churches, but they are particularly tragic in the very small congregations. As the church becomes larger, the clan problem declines in importance unless the family groups form coalitions over certain issues, at which point the resolution of the issue in question is probably more important than the family structure of the people involved. As a church grows beyond the clan-dominated stage, the problem of growth is more associated with a feeling of satisfaction on the part of the congregation and of organizational inertia on the part of the pastor and his staff.

The church with 120 in attendance has learned that the pastor cannot lead his congregation alone, and that the church building must remain open for business all through the week. A church at this size is large enough that it can pay its pastor a fair salary, provide a parsonage, and offer the community a nice church building with a good public image. The pastor surrounds himself with a group of lay workers. He puts in office hours, and may have a part-time church secretary (probably his wife at no extra pay!). With this many people, there are enough musicians to play the piano and organ well, and someone knows how to develop an acceptable choir.

One of the limiting factors of the church at 120 is that much of its work is done by lay people with very little training. They enjoy doing what they do, but they feel inferior in the presence of anyone with professional experience. They are not capable of causing growth and they are not apt to ask for help. The church is large enough for their purposes, and they have just enough new people coming in to replace those who move away or leave them for other churches. Potentially, however, the church at 120 is in a good position for further expansion, if it can dare to make its administrative and ministerial changes and have the faith for a suitable building.

The changes that must be made at 120 are mostly adequate for continued growth until the congregation reaches the mid 200s or early 300s. By that time the congregation will have hired a full-time secretary and established an efficient church office with a wide range of services to the pastor, the congregation, and the community. The Sunday school is departmentalized, and is directed and taught by a well-trained staff of Christian laymen. In the pulpit, the pastor has ceased to chat informally with his congregation as though he were having coffee in their living rooms, and he is truly preaching sermons with significant style and content. He has sufficient help from competent laymen that he can give adequate time and effort to his sermon preparation.

Most pastors hire assistant pastors much too soon. Until a church reaches 250 to 300, the church would do well to hire janitorial help to free the pastor from the physical upkeep of the church properties and competent secretarial help to support the pastor with an efficient office. It seems to me that most pastors with less that 250 in attendance do not know what to do with assistant pastors. They generally put them over youth and music, and then have to do all the administrative work themselves. The church cannot afford the salary of a good secretary, so the assistant pastor's wife is asked to work in the office. She resents having to do office work for no additional salary, so she does not do well even if she is capable. The pastor does not treat her as a secretary because he feels she is doing him a favor by working in the office. As a result, the pastor increases his worry and his workload. It is better to set up an efficient church office with one or more qualified secretarial workers until the church is larger. Furthermore, by so doing the pastor learns how to manage an office staff before he begins to bring in other ministers to work under his direction.

It is very difficult for a church to break out of the format that produces a congregation of 250 to 300. It is a very stable period, because the church is large enough to be considered impressively large and small enough to be thought of as comfortably small. Everyone still may know everyone else, yet the structure is not so tightly set that new people cannot enter the social circle. The pastor is getting a good salary. The church can pay all its own bills. The facilities are nice. Unless the pastor and his congregation catch a vision of their task in their community and world, they will remain at this comfortable stage forever.

To go beyond the 250 to 300 stage requires a different kind of organization, for this is the upper limit of what one pastor can do with a group of willing laymen and an efficient office. To break out of this stage and grow on up to the next level at 400, 600, or 800, the church must add to its ministerial staff. By the time a church reaches this level of growth it can afford the necessary salaries, no matter what may be said to the contrary.

What a church does as it grows out of the 200s is vitally important. At this point it can develop its base of administration and ministry in stages and therefore grow in stages that will level off at just under 400, under 600, under 800, and under 1,200; or, it can envision its needs for a church of 1,200 and expand its base of administration sufficiently to develop a steady growth rate up to that figure. Most churches take the first alternative because they cannot form a mental image of their church at a size much larger than its present level. The only difference, other than basic faith and creative planning, is in how soon the staff can be enlarged.

The next step after providing janatorial services and organizing an efficient office with good secretarial help is to add a second minister to the staff. He should not be merely an assistant to the pastor, but a fully recognized minister who will help to pastor the church under the direction of the executive pastor. Although he may work with the portfolio of youth minister or minister of music, he also should share in the administrative burden of the church office and in the responsibilities of visitation and evangelism. Clearly defined lines of authority and responsibility will remove any competitive feelings between members of the staff.

By the time the church reaches 600 in attendance, it must have ministers of youth, music, Christian education, and visitation in addition to its executive pastor. Further limitation factors will be removed by providing these men and women with adequate office help. The minister of youth will usually be a young man himself, often recently out of theology school. The minister of music should be a professional at church music who not only can lead the choirs and orchestras, but knows how to develop and train a wide range of musical and artistic talent in the whole congregation. The Christian education minister must be either a theological minister who specializes in education or an educator who feels called to the ministry. The visitation minister often is an older pastor who joins the staff of a larger church after years of experience. This is an excellent opportunity for an older minister who has much ministerial experience to offer, but does not feel he can continue with the full load of a pastorate.

The barrier at 1,200 is to church growth what the sound barrier is to flight. A different set of rules apply beyond that point. Few congregations have learned how to organize a church with more than 1,200, and there are not enough examples around to establish where the numerical barriers are beyond that level. It does appear that beyond 1,200 to 1,400 in attendance a church must go into a very different form of organization and social concept than was required at any previous stage.

To go back to our working model of the sand pyramid on the table, there comes a time when merely expanding the base by adding more surface to the table is not enough. The table itself will collapse under the weight of the increasing mass unless we bring in some engineers and design a new kind of table. I feel that a church reaches this critical point at about 1,200 to 1,400 in attendance.

It appears that this size of church must take on some of the characteristics of a corporation. It not only must increase its ministerial and secretarial staff, but it must also hire a business administrator who frees the ministers for the spiritual services of the church. The dynamics of the congregation itself change considerably once the number is too large for any member to know all the other members. The pastors would have to provide a wide variety of services to appeal to many different kinds of people. The congregation would begin to form small units clustered about topics and services of different interests. The church must resist the temptation to let its members become lost in the crowd, for once they become mere spectators instead of participants, the death knell begins to toll for any further growth. In my own experience, when I reached this stage I divided the congregation into teams and started a number of new churches all through the city of Bogota, Colombia. The church remained at about 1,000, but the total outreach of the congregation was 3,000 to 4,000 every Sunday, some of the people in the main church and others in house meetings.

Here in America we have a few large churches in the thousands of adherents now, and I believe we will see more and more churches move into growth patterns in excess of 2,500 and even larger. No doubt there is a level at which it will no longer be practical to build larger and larger sanctuaries with more and more massive educational wings. However, at the present time there are too few examples of such churches to know just where that limit of practicality might be.

So far, our working model provides only for growing congregations meeting in traditional sanctuaries. The great majority of our churches are not ready for anything more than this. We must remember, however, that the task of the church is worship, teaching apostolic doctrine and experience, fellowship, and total world evangelization. If the church remains task-oriented, it eventually must adopt methods of evangelization that may carry it far afield from its sanctuary-oriented mode.

I can envision a church with tens of thousands of adherents pervading a whole community, yet all under one congregational system with one executive pastor and a large number of ministerial workers. It would meet mostly in houses, but would revolve around a focal motivational and training center. It would have a large auditorium for mass evangelistic rallies, gospel music concerts, and divine healing meetings. The motivation would come not only from these worship and evangelistic centers, but would result from a massive training program to offer a wide range of Christian education. In effect, we would drop the limited concepts of the traditional Sunday school and turn the whole church into a lay Bible school. This motivational and training center would be the hub around which would revolve an unlimited number of house meetings at any hour of the day or night, reaching out and enveloping a large segment of the local community.

Such dreams are still far beyond the reach of most American congregations. The present need is to catch a vision of the dynamic relationship between their administrative base and their numerical mass, and to make the right decisions to establish a continuous growth pattern.

One of the most effective ways to expand the administrative base of a church is to make wise use of the church board of deacons. The deacons are called by various names in different churches, but most American congregations have some kind of central committee of laymen. They can be a wonderful asset to the church, but they can also become a much too conservative force. The wise pastor will offer leadership training for his board members and will give to each of them a separate task or portfolio. Let each member of the board become the chairman of a committee so that he will be influenced by a broad base of congregational opinion, and so a large number of people will become involved in the decision-making processes.

I have observed many churches, but I have never yet seen a congregation develop satisfactorily for long if its pastor was not the leader of the church and the chairman of the board. In New Testament times, the deacons were chosen to assist the ministers, not to be a board of directors over them. One deacon told me, "Pastors may come and go, but the church goes on." I would not pastor a church if I could not be its leader, and I would not advise any pastor to accept such a position of nonbiblical organization.

While I believe that the pastor should be in charge of the congregation, I also know that the pastor and his attitude often are the conservative elements that limit the growth of a church. To lead a congregation and develop it into a living and growing force in the community, a pastor and his helpers must be creative people who are not afraid to consider the alternatives to their present methods and to maintain a dynamic interaction between their growing number of believers and their administrative and ministerial operation.

In northern El Salvador, I once stood at the base of an ancient Mayan pyramid. I was amazed to see that this very old structure was built upon the ruins of an even older pyramid beneath it.

It is never too late to make a church grow. Even with the most unlikely congregation, we can build upon the ruins of the past and take the church into a new era of successful development. According to the Pyramid Principle, we must first lay out the structural base, and then we may expect to build up the mass with a new addition of Christian converts.

6

A Miracle Every Sunday

The jet airplane taxied up to the main terminal at San Francisco and shut down the mighty engines that had brought me halfway across the nation from Kansas City. Soon I was walking up the enclosed ramp and looking into the faces of the people who had come to meet the passengers.

Two young men of Mexican heritage stepped out of the crowd and said, "*Hermano* David?"

I asked, "How did you recognize me?"

"That was easy," one of them told me. "We said '*Hermano* David' to everybody, and you were the only one who answered."

It seemed reasonable enough.

I had been invited to be the main speaker for an annual conference of Spanish-speaking churches from all over the West Coast and was looking forward to preaching again in my second language. Within a few hours I would address more than 2,000 *hermanos* in San Jose's civic auditorium.

As we drove along the freeway to San Jose, I learned that both of these young ministers had recently graduated from a Spanish Bible college at La Puente, California, and were now in their first months of ministry. They had offered to drive to San Francisco to get me so they could ask how to make their little churches grow. Both of them had accepted the sort of churches that are always offered to new Bible school graduates—small, in debt, and desperate. I felt sorry for them, but I knew they must cut their teeth on adversity if they were ever to amount to anything for God. My own first pastorate was at Union Gap, Washington, where I had to drive a meat truck to support my wife and two babies and still try to pastor the church. People used to tease me about peddling baloney all week and preaching on Sunday!

What can you tell two young men who have not yet proved the basics of pastoring, far less become ready for advanced concepts of church growth?

I said, "Do everything they taught you in Bible school, and then have a miracle happen every Sunday."

They seemed enthusiastic over this wonderful advice, but I could tell they were waiting for more.

I opened my Spanish Bible and read to them from *San Mateo* (Saint Matthew) 9:35. Our English Bible says, "And Jesus went about all the cities and villages, teaching in their synagogues, and preaching the gospel of the kingdom, and healing every sickness and every disease among the people."

I told them they should do the same things Jesus did in all the cities and villages. They should teach in the house of God, preach the gospel to the masses, and believe God for the healing of the people. Through the channel of Christian ministry, God has provided belief for man's mind, inspiration and guidance for his life in society, and healing for his spirit and body. I told these young pastors that they must minister to all the needs of men if they want their churches to grow. I said, "If you feed the sheep, the sheep will come to you."

We have said that the task of a church is to worship God, preserve and teach apostolic doctrine and experience, provide fellowship for believers, and evangelize its community and its world. Each part of this task is open ground for the three ministries of teaching, preaching, and working miracles.

The difference between teaching and preaching is not so much in the content of the materials as in the style of delivery. The art of teaching is intended for a thinking audience. It is the mode of communication we choose when we have a well-polarized group of people who are willing to think with us in logical sequences. With such a group we can explain the doctrines of the church and educate the people about the Christian life. Teaching can be inspirational and very exciting, but it will always have the characteristic of rationality.

We can truly teach only those people who by a willful act of the mind open themselves up to us and allow themselves to think with us in rational patterns. Ordinarily, logical thinking is possible only to individuals in small control groups. However, a good speaker can polarize the minds of a congregation into a sort of rationality. The effect is never total in a congregation, but by mastering the art of capturing and holding the attention of an audience a speaker can communicate with a congregation on a somewhat rational plane.

Teaching is a rational approach to the communication of ideas, with an objective to educate the hearers and produce alterations in their opinions and behavior.

Preaching, on the other hand, is an intuitive method. Like an artist's painting, it communicates beyond the level of words by expressing emotions, opinions, and intuitive knowledge. Preaching is not necessarily irrational or illogical, but it does not depend on ordered sequences of thought for its method of expression. Preaching reaches into the heart of man and convinces him that what the speaker has to say is right . . . whether or not he understands it!

Preaching alone is incomplete. Teaching alone lacks the motivational impact to move large numbers of people at one time, and therefore is insufficient. The two forms of Christian communication complement one another and are each essential to the other.

Man in the general masses or in random groups is not rational. He lives at an intuitive level where he is moved by affirmative or negative reactions to the world about him. He does not understand the sun; he just reacts to its warmth and has good feelings about it. If most people would listen to a logical explanation of the thermonuclear conversion of hydrogen into helium that makes the energy production of the sun possible, they would be bored to tears. People live at an intuitive level by choice; they do not want to think logically. When they were preschool children they tried to figure out everything about the universe, but by the time they were old enough to find some of the answers to their earlier questions they already had decided the world could not be explained in a rational way. Their minds are like computers already programmed incorrectly, and now they reject the analysis of a problem and choose rather to tell us how they feel about a subject. It is not so much that they are irrational as that they choose to reject rationality in favor of intuition and opinion.

This nonthinking approach to life is one of blind reactions to opinions and the chemical production of their own glands. An affirmative or negative feeling about a thing or a generous spurt of adrenalin into the body is a more convincing argument than the most well-researched rational presentation.

I do not mean to sell the human race short. Individual persons certainly are capable of incisive, logical thinking. Yet, they seldom live up to their innate potential. When they form groups or act *en masse*, they always sacrifice logic and their individual freedom in favor of a sort of community or crowd consciousness.

The advertising field has learned this lesson well. Advertisers do not appeal to their prospective customers on a rational plane. They seek an emotional response based on acceptance or rejection of their appeal. The packaging of products comes about from in-depth studies in motivational research. For example, catfoods must appeal to people, not to cats. Their flavors must remain in the human-pleasing range of fish, chicken, and beef. No sensitive owner would buy his dear kitten a catfood flavored with mouse, grasshopper, or sparrow.

Yes, the masses are irrational. They do not think in logical sequences, but in intuitive reactions based on the opinions of their minds and the organic plumbing system of their bodies. Furthermore, they tend to cluster their affirmative and negative responses around certain mental images and symbols.

Jesus knew this. That is why He usually preached to the multitudes in parables. He gave them mental images around which they could gather their affirmative and negative feelings and their intuitive opinions. By hanging His preaching on the memory pegs of images from their own lives, He gave structure to their accumulated opinions and turned them from a disordered mass into an army of dedicated followers. Only later with His smaller control group of disciples did He go into detail to explain His parables. When He spoke in images to the masses, He was preaching; and when He explained His ideas to His disciples, he was teaching. Both methods of communication were necessary to His purpose.

Preaching, then, is a mode of communication to the intuitive masses. It draws on the emotional reserve of the speaker and expresses his thoughts in a setting of intuitive acceptance or rejection of the message and the messenger. Its purpose is to move men to action, especially that of accepting Jesus Christ as Savior and Lord.

There should be no conflict between the two verbal forms. They are two different tools in the hands of the minister and the lay gospel worker to reach people wherever they are and bring them into the kingdom of God. Matthew said of Jesus, "But when he saw the multitudes, he was moved with compassion on them, because they fainted, and were scattered abroad, as sheep having no shepherd" (Matt. 9:36). He later said to one of His disciples, "Feed my sheep" (John

21:16). Jesus recognized this deep separation of the rational and irrational mentality of men, and He made a difference in His presentations to the sheep and the shepherds. What this means for a local congregation is that it must reach its community on both levels. A church must offer the very best in Christian education, appealing to the rational minds of the community with clearly defined explanations of Christian doctrine, experience, and practice. At the same time, it must follow the example of Jesus by offering a compassionate ministry to the popular masses of intuitive men. The only way a church can thoroughly reach its community and its world is to utilize the whole range of human intellect and emotions—to reach every man where he is and bring him into the fold.

There will be times, however, when nothing seems to work. We explain the Christian faith to the best of our ability, and still men do not seem to understand. We need some added element to give credibility to our message. We tell men that God created the world and all that is in it, that He can do anything if we just ask Him. We tell them how Jesus went about healing the sick and casting out devils. Meanwhile, our hearers are suffering from nervous tensions, physical disorders, and a whole range of life's needs. We can talk about the power of God only so long before we must offer some practical demonstration of God's miraculous ability to heal. It is precisely at this point that the Christian religion may prove its exclusive superiority over all other forms of religion or nonreligion.

The Bible teaches us emphatically that God hears and answers prayer. Jesus said, "If ye shall ask anything in my name, I will do it" (John 14:14). The promise sounds almost too good to be true. Must we qualify His promise, or did He really mean what He said?

James, a son of Mary and Joseph and therefore half-brother to Jesus, wrote, "And the prayer of faith shall save the sick, and the Lord shall raise him up" (James 5:15).

Such biblical passages are much too explicit to be taken figuratively or passed off as the overly enthusiastic statements of first-century writers.

The apostle John did qualify the promise a little by saying that our petitions should be according to God's will. He said, "These things have I written unto you that believe on the name of the Son of God; that ye may know that ye have eternal life, and that ye may believe on the name of the Son of God. And this is the confidence that we have in him, that, if we ask any thing according to his will, he heareth us: and if we know that he hears us, whatsoever we ask, we know that we have the petitions that we desired of him" (1 John 5:13-15).

It is clearly taught in the New Testament that God hears the prayers of those who believe on Jesus Christ, and that, if our petitions are consistent with His will, He will answer our prayers.

I agree with Dr. Harold Lindsell, editor-publisher of *Christianity Today* magazine, who said in his book *When You Pray*, "We assert boldly that God answers prayer and that prayer releases the mighty power of God. But if no prayers are answered and no power manifested, then the theory remains unproven or falls to the ground. But if it can be shown that prayers are answered and power manifested, then we must conclude that prayer works in practice and is more than just a theory. Certainly we must face the pragmatic test when we propound the theory that God answers prayer and ask the all-important question, 'Does it really work in practice?' " (Published by Tyndale House Publishers, Wheaton, Illinois: 1969, pp. 134-135.)

The claim that God hears and answers prayer is at the very heart of the Christian religion. If we can promise our community and our world that men can talk with God and that God will reply to their individual requests, then we can boldly go to any man anywhere and tell him the good news. As Dr. Lindsell said, the key question is: Does it work?

The answer of millions of Christians through the ages attests to the validity of prayer. Many miracles have happened in the past, and they continue to occur today. The continuing proof of this claim is so basic to Christianity that without it the whole religion fails. I can add my own testimony to the witness of Christians everywhere that I regularly talk with God and that my whole life has been a continuous chain of prayer-answered events.

One cannot limit the power of prayer or the kinds of petitions that God will honor, except that the requests must be consistent with His will as contained in the Bible. I have made some observations, however, that might help the novice to understand the conditions in which prayer is most often answered.

First, God does not generally give a new reply if He has already specifically provided for the request in His Word. For example, if you pray for the Lord to be with you, you do not need and probably will not receive a specific sign of His presence. The reason for this is that Jesus has already told you, "Lo, I am with you alway, even unto the end of the world" (Matt. 28:20). It is very important that those who pray also become well acquainted with the Scriptures.

Second, the Lord often uses His Word to reply to our requests. When a Christian believer has a problem in understanding some situation or why certain things have happened to him, he is very apt to hear the pastor preach a sermon on that topic or hear someone discuss the same problem on a gospel radio or television program. The phenomenon happens too often to be coincidental.

Third, God often uses people to respond to the prayers of a Christian believer. If you are in need of food and you pray, "Give us this day our daily bread," you should not be surprised if somebody comes by your house and gives you a gift of food. The donor may not even know that he is answering prayer, but may just think he is being kind to someone in need. Again, the Lord might answer your prayer for bread by having someone offer you a job or give you a raise in pay. Answers to prayer seldom seem supernatural at the moment of their arrival.

Fourth, the Lord seldom gives us anything we do not need. For this reason, well-fed, satisfied people do not often see supernatural events happen about them. This apparently is part of what John meant by saying we must ask according to God's will. As long as men have any other resource than that of prayer, they tend to trust first in all the other alternatives. Evangelistic sermons abound with fantastic promises that lead people to believe that the signs of faith in God are a large bank account, a luxurious car, and a huge house. Nothing could be farther from the truth; for God has promised to supply our needs, not our whims or our greed.

Fifth, God is more apt to heal something that has gone wrong in nature than to break His natural laws for your personal benefit. The Scriptures abound with promises that God will heal a broken body or a broken spirit. In fact, every evangelical church has members who have been miraculously healed of some serious sickness. Divine healing is such a common occurrence in gospel-preaching churches that most cases are never reported outside the local congregations. The great majority of such healings are the correction of something that has gone wrong in nature, rather than the breaking of God's universal laws. For example, the Lord might heal you of cancer; but He is not apt to grant your request to whisk you off to take a close look at the Planet Pluto. He might heal a withered hand; but He probably will not grow you an extra one.

Sixth, the Lord did not give us miracles to replace normal human activities, but rather to prove His existence and the validity of His gospel. He gives us just enough miracles for us to know He is with us, and just few enough to keep us actively engaged with the normal range of human life. If we pray for divine healing, He is just as apt to take us successfully through surgery as He is to give us an instantaneous cure. Only He knows what we really need. Thus, we do not express a lack of faith by going to a doctor or entering a hospital for care. We pray and put ourselves in His hands, and we trust Him to do what is best for us, knowing that He always hears us and always answers.

Seventh, miracles tend to occur along the cutting edge of evangelization. Because the principal purpose of God in doing miracles is to prove His existence and the validity of His gospel, we should expect a greater concentration of miracles when we are attempting to prove the reality of God and the truth of His message than when we are carrying out other activities of the church. This in fact is the observation of many people deeply involved in evangelization.

God once answered my prayer to send rain on a South American village. The people had not had rain in some weeks and were in danger of losing their annual crops of coffee, sugar cane, and pineapples. When the new Christian converts in the village asked me to pray for rain, I did so; and the rains came that night. The Lord taught those new converts (and me) a valuable lesson, but I am sure He never intended that I should go around upsetting the normal weather elsewhere. Miracles, then, tend to happen in the context of the convert-making work of the church. This explains why the more evangelistic churches report more miracles than do the less evangelistically oriented churches.

The Bible teaches this connection between miracles and evangelism. When asked to prove the validity of His contact with the Father, Jesus offered answered prayer as one of His proofs. He said, "He that believeth on me, the works that I do shall he do also; and greater works than these shall he do; because I go unto my Father. And whatsoever ye shall ask in my name, that will I do, that the Father may be glorified in the Son" (John 14:12-13). Jesus intended that answered prayer would be a major proof of the reality of the Christian religion.

One of the problems we face whenever we discuss miracles is that there are so many religious quacks who promise divine healing as proof of their message. A good question to ask when confronted by possible religious quackery is: Who receives the glory? If the credit for the healing goes to Jesus Christ and His gospel, then you should not oppose the person or his ministry; for we must always leave room for unique events and unique, even eccentric, people. However, if the glory of the event centers around some person and the flaunting of his special gifts, you should suspect false doctrine and separate yourself from its influence. It would be interesting to hear such people preach on the text: "Not unto us, O Lord, not unto us, but unto thy name give glory, for thy mercy, and for thy truth's sake" (Ps. 115:1).

Jesus' response to the multitudes of His day was to teach, preach, and work miracles. For the even larger multitudes of our day we must go back to the original methods of Jesus and apply them to our community and our world.

Church growth is not an end in itself, nor may its aspirations be separated from all the other goals of the Body of Christ in the world. The church is one, and its purpose is one—to put the hands of a growing number of people into the hand of God. To accomplish such a task, we must reach all men where they are, be it at a rational or an intuitive plane, and prove our verbal message with demonstrable answers to prayer. We cannot say that teaching, preaching, and miracles will in themselves produce church growth; but we must say that without the motivation of communicating the gospel to men and establishing bonds of faith and interaction between men and God the whole subject of church growth has little meaning.

Yes, I believe I advised those young ministers correctly: Do everything they taught you in Bible school, and then have a miracle every Sunday.

7
The Cutting Edge

I am convinced that of all the sciences the most difficult is theology—the science of religious belief. The researcher in any other science dedicates himself to an increasing specialization, narrowing his field of study until he knows a great amount about a single aspect of his subject. The fellow who starts out to be a biologist successively becomes a zoologist, then an entomologist, and finally makes his name as the world's leading authority on the nervous system of the tsetse fly.

It is not so in theology. In "the queen of the sciences" the theologian must learn more and more about more and more, ever expanding his understanding to envelop and pervade every other discipline of the mind until finally he grasps toward the sum total of human knowledge and includes it all in his cosmic system. Any theological conclusion must either take in all known truth or be counted as error.

Much as doctrinal error results from a limited vision and an ignorance of vital factors, so the failure to achieve church growth may be caused by too narrow a frame of reference. Schopenhauer said, "Every man takes the limit of his own field of vision for the limit of the world." Ultimately, every one of us is enclosed by the limitations of our own ideas, for we cannot go beyond our own degree of comprehension. Confronted by our own lack of constructive concepts, we are like the Samaritan woman who spoke of having "nothing to draw with, and the well is deep" (John 4:11). Or, perhaps we are like the woman in Chaucer's *Canterbury Tales* of whom the Old English author wrote, "A yard she had, enclosed all about with sticks, and a dry ditch without."

The limits of what we can do for God are the outer peripheries of our own creative ability to see what is not yet there and to believe what is not yet come to pass. "Now faith is the substance of things hoped for, the evidence of things not seen" (Heb. 11:1). For a world that does not yet exist, and for conditions we do not yet fully comprehend, we look to the future and declare bravely that our churches will grow. We create our next stages by faith, and then we boldly step forward and make our faith a reality.

There are those who have questioned my approach to theology as well as my views on church growth. Some have complained of my apparent lack of structure, formula, or even an outline. The charge is unfounded, of course; it is only that I try to put enough flesh on the bones of my subject that its every joint and connecting tendon do not show through a thin-skinned surface. Many theological writers construct a subject as though it were a series of building blocks, each block logically following the one before it. In this manner, the reader learns only about the surface of things. I tend rather to bore into the very heart of the matter (Oh, how true!) and then explore the subject from the inside. As I work my way through the internal complications of the topic, I run into many turns and surprises; but I discover a lot about my subject that the structure people never learn. While such writers describe a pyramid by taking you on a step-by-step climb to its rocky top, I take you down into the inner passageways where we can explore the hidden chambers withheld from the common eye. It is sometimes obscure, but that is one of the hazards of following me through the inside of a subject.

Before you can be creative in any field, you must read widely and think deeply in that field. This is true for the theologian, but it is also true for anyone who wants to make a church grow. A congregation that wants to increase its effectiveness and grow to a larger influence in the community should find out what other churches are doing. Its leaders should read the many church-growth books now on the market. It should name special study committees and put the whole church to thinking about alternative ways of doing things. We must never be afraid of change, only for change for which we are unprepared.

One of our limitation factors in church growth is the ambiguity in our definition of evangelism. Just about everyone who wants to prove the religious worth of his program says his work is evangelistic. A whole branch of Protestant theology calls itself evangelical. Furthermore, a person cannot read the Saturday newspapers without seeing that certain ministers call themselves evangelists. Yet, in spite of the common usage of these *evangel* words, most churchgoers cannot explain the difference between evangelism and evangelization.

All of these words come from the Greek work *euaggelion,* translated into English as "gospel" or "good news." It is used in the New Testament to refer to the central core of Christian truth about the death and resurrection of Jesus Christ and the related doctrines of personal salvation and eternal life. This central essence of Christianity, sometimes called the *kerygma* because it was the basic message preached by the first-century apostles, is the good news that God became man to forgive our sins and show us the way to heaven. Specifically, it means the proclamation of the gospel to the world, and it generally includes the task of making converts and establishing congregations of believers in churches.

Perhaps it would help if we could see the main *euaggelion* words together:

Evangelize (verb) is to proclaim the gospel.

Evangelism (noun) is the proclamation of the gospel.

Evangelization (noun) is the act of proclaiming the gospel.

Evangelist (noun) is a person who proclaims the gospel, especially as a vocation.

Evangelistic (adjective) refers to anything related to the proclamation of the gospel.

Evangelical (adjective) refers to persons or churches who proclaim the gospel, especially those who take a theological position on the subject.

Typical of the misuse of these words is the ambiguity between evangelism and evangelization. While the former may refer to any subject related to the proclamation of the gospel, the latter may be used only to describe the very act of the proclamation itself. Quite often, evangelism is talking about the subject, while evangelization is doing something about it.

One of the afflictions of our age is the tendency to live at a secondary level of discussion and documentation rather than at a primary level of action and fulfillment. We have become a society of spectators, not of participants. We sit by the millions around our television sets while a few chosen athletes perform for our entertainment. The active participants experience the deeply emotional effects of joy and sorrow, while tragically the secondary spectators accept victory or defeat with a mere turn of the television dial. The difference between the muscle and bone of the real world and the make-believe fantasies of the glass screen are so great that we are in danger of mass cultural withdrawal from primary experience.

Every time we turn around today, someone is announcing another conference or seminar on evangelism. More and more colleges are including studies on evangelism in their curricula, and many doctoral candidates are writing dissertations on past evangelistic efforts. Few real evangelists are writing on the subject, and few who write on the subject are real evangelists. No one will ever know how many spontaneous outbursts of evangelization have received their only structured methodology on the pages of some church publication or college report. Hungry magazine editors and students gobble up the news of evangelistic efforts, much as sports writers analyze a sports event for months after its occurrence.

The real tragedy is that the secondary level of talking and writing about evangelism begins to affect the primary evangelization itself. Evangelists, impressed by the promotional value of magazines and documentary pictures, begin to arrange their activities to produce the best possible photographs and make the best stories for publication. The purpose of the primary event becomes the feeding of data to the secondary level of documentation. The demands of the spectators determine the next moves of the participants.

Imagine a gigantic field of ripened grain with windblown waves surging across its surface as though it were an ocean turned golden by the sunset. Although the sun is going down and storm clouds are heaped upon the horizon, only a small corner of the field has yet been harvested. In the foreground a crowd of potential reapers is seated on the ground listening to a leading expert on methods of harvesting speak to them on how far from the soil level one should strike with the sickle. It is all very inspirational, but a stormy night is coming and the precious grain will be lost.

We have had enough talk about evangelism; it is time to plunge into the primary task of actual evangelization. We must thrust in the sickle and bring in the sheaves of golden grain before it is forever too late.

Jesus said to His disciples, "The harvest truly is plenteous, but the labourers are few; pray ye therefore the Lord of the harvest, that he will send forth labourers into his harvest" (Matt. 9:37-38).

Evangelization is to the Christian laborer what the sickle is to the reaper. The followers of Christ must depart from the comforts of their traditional sanctuaries and go forth into the ripened fields to bring in the sheaves of waiting men. The time for talking is past; it is now time for dedicated workers to arise with determination for the final culmination of the harvest. "They that sow in tears shall reap in joy.

He that goeth forth and weepeth, bearing precious seed, shall doubtless come again with rejoicing, bringing his sheaves with him" (Ps. 126:5-6).

Three actions are required of the reaper.

First, he must thrust in the sickle. The decisive contact of the gospel with a human life brings the person being evangelized into a vital crisis in which he must accept or reject Jesus Christ and His message. True evangelization is not some vague influence in society brought about by charitable institutions and other humanitarian efforts; it is a direct confrontation of men with the claims of Jesus Christ. The church must face men squarely with the truth of the gospel, much as a reaper takes a decisive swing with his scythe.

Jesus Christ either (a) is or (b) is not God revealed to men. He either (c) did or (d) did not rise from the dead. The gospel either (e) is or (f) is not true. People who believe in Jesus Christ either (g) are or (h) are not forgiven of their sins and saved from the wrath of God. The children of the Lord either (i) will or (j) will not live forever in heaven. Christianity is a decisive religion that demands a clear set of choices, and it sends out its evangelists to confront every man with its message and bring people to a point of critical determination for or against Jesus Christ.

The second action of the reaper is to tie the sheaves. There are few things in this world more beautiful or nostalgic to man than a well-tied bundle of newly harvested grain. It represents the reward of a long season of waiting on the slow sun and the reluctant rain, of watching the green shoots break through the soil and rise to the full development of life-giving seeds. A sheaf of grain represents the promise of continued human life. It must be gathered in the arms and tied securely without losing a single kernel of wheat.

The proclamation of the gospel without the individual follow-up of establishing converts in churches is irresponsible. Random evangelistic efforts without gathering in the converts in groups for a continued Christian influence under the watchful care of the church is like bringing children into the world without offering them the love and protection of a family and home. The reaper who thrusts in the sickle and demands the commitment of the harvest must not leave the grain to spoil on the ground, but must gather it into his arms and tie it into the sheaves of the church.

The reaper's third action is to bring the sheaves into the barn. Once the grain has felt the sickle and been tied in bundles, it must be brought into the storehouse where it may feed the world on its life-giving bread. The end result of evangelization is to produce spiritual food to feed a hungry world.

A church must remain along the cutting edge of evangelization if it is to fulfill its divine task. It is along this sickle-sharp edge of converting lost men that the living Christ has promised to be present with His church, for it was only after He said, "Go ye therefore, and teach all nations," that He said, "Lo, I am with you alway, even unto the end of the world" (Matt. 28:19-20).

No church is truly Christian that does not engage in an active search for converts, both in its own community and in the unevangelized nations of the world.

Locally, a congregation may at times carry out special evangelistic activities such as revival campaigns, door-to-door witnessing, or visitation programs, but the principal soul-winning ministries of the church will result from the total impact of the lives of the members in the community. People who have been helped by the church and its contact with Jesus Christ will in turn talk with other friends and relatives who need similar assistance. A combination of inspiration and efficiency in the church and an open attitude of personal witnessing among the congregation will produce a steady flow of converts.

In addition, each local church should support the work of its denomination to spread over its own nation. It should help sponsor new churches in undeveloped areas and assist both with finances and with personnel.

There are three ways a local church may support the cause of foreign missions. First, it can pray for its missionaries and their effectiveness in other lands. Second, it can encourage its own young people to enter the Christian ministry and follow the leading of the Lord to foreign service. And, third, it can dedicate its financial support to the work of foreign missions.

How much of its budget should a local church give to the missionary endeavors outside its own immediate community? That will depend, of course, upon the degree of importance a congregation places on the evangelization of the world. If a church believes that all the world must hear the gospel before the return of Jesus Christ, then it will make its foreign missions outreach a major project. According to the Olivet Discourse (Matthew 24), the completion of the worldwide witness of the church may be the only remaining prophecy to be fulfilled before the Second Coming of Christ. Can it be that the primary cause of God in the world should ever become a secondary cause in His church?

God has promised to bless those who give liberally to His cause. The apostle Paul wrote to the Corinthians, "He which soweth sparingly shall reap also sparingly; and he which soweth bountifully shall reap also bountifully. Every man according as he purposeth in his heart, so let him give; not grudgingly, or of necessity: for God loveth a cheerful giver. And God is able to make all grace abound toward you; that ye, always having all sufficiency in all things, may abound to every good work" (2 Cor. 9:6-8).

There is no question about it: God blesses a missionary church. The church that is not deeply involved in the cause of world evangelization should give some consideration to the fact that the largest, most rapidly growing churches are those which give the most to foreign missions. Do they give large amounts of money to missions because they are big enough to do so, or did they become large because of their missionary involvement? The latter point seems to be correct.

We may think of the church budget as comprised of four sections. Each congregation has its own personality and circumstances, but yet its budget will tend to fall into the general categories of salaries, buildings and maintenance, ministries and services, and world missions. No church should ever give less then 10 percent of its total income to missions, and to call itself a missionary church in the true sense it should give 25 to 30 percent. For any people who take the commands of Jesus Christ seriously, the Great Commission is an inescapable challenge that demands a significant part of their church's attention.

Those who are not accustomed to this degree of missionary involvement will probably not understand when I say that the more money a church gives away the more it will prosper. People want to belong to a meaningful church that is doing something effective to help their world; and the more a church contributes to the missionary cause the more the members will support the other programs of the church.

What kind of missionary work should a local church support? There are many programs that crowd under the umbrella of foreign missions, just as there are many who claim to be evangelistic. Some organizations are sincere but ineffective, while some others are dishonest fund raisers who are protected by the great distances to far-off orphanages, literature programs, and Bible-smuggling operations. Some organizations spend much of their income on administration, with just enough of a foreign program to produce pictures and articles for their magazines.

There are several things you need to know. First, you should support the missionary program of your own denomination. All of the fastest growing foreign churches are sponsored by or are in close fellowship with worldwide organized church movements. Such denominations as the Assemblies of God, the Southern Baptists, the Christian and Missionary Alliance, the Presbyterians, the Methodists, and other such Protestant churches account for the great majority of effective missionary work going on in the world today. In addition, some interdenominational organizations such as the Sudan Interior Mission, Africa Inland Missions, the Latin American Mission, and others of this nature who draw their personnel and support from denominational sources are doing an effective job.

Second, you should support the kind of missionary work that makes converts to Jesus Christ and establishes them in congregations of believers. Place your first priority on the building of the Body of Christ in other lands.

Third, there are certain auxiliary mission-related programs that are worthy of the church's support. You should ask the missionary leaders of your own denomination which of these are most helpful to your own missionaries. Organizations such as the American Bible Society, who make the Bible available in many lands, and the Wycliffe Bible Translators, who go into tribal areas and reduce the languages to writing for Bible translation, are indispensable to missionary work.

Ideally, each church should send its young people into Christian ministry and encourage them to go into foreign missionary service. Any church that sends out its own flesh and blood to the mission fields will have no problem in knowing where to put its missionary funds.

The important point is that every congregation must live and breathe for no other cause than the worship of God, the teaching of apostolic doctrine and experience, the fellowship of Christian believers, and the evangelization of the world. The church exists for the harvest and its reapers. On the local scene, it must continuously bring in new converts; and in other lands it must supply and support foreign missionaries who will in turn establish growing churches.

Yes, the task of world evangelization is difficult, because it requires the total commitment of all those who believe in its accomplishment. The world is a waiting field of ripened grain. We must thrust in the sickle and bring the sheaves into the shelter of the Lord.

8

In Touch with the Spirit World

No matter how much we may speak of the church in terms of numerical growth, administrative organization, and evangelistic expansion over the earth, we must finally admit that none of these human activities are of lasting value without a living contact with the world of spirit. The ultimate duty of the church is to put the hands of men into the hand of God.

At the serious mention of the spirit world, most people express an uneasy feeling of mixed curiosity and fear. A few of the more mystically minded hearers will ask questions about the occult or extrasensory perception, but the majority of men will not probe into an unseen dimension outside their own secure world. Old tribal fears are still too near the surface of most modern men to allow them to discuss the spirit world objectively or to allow themselves to experience any willful contact with that mysterious realm beyond the normal range of their senses.

Most of us do not realize how very thin is the barrier we have placed between our consciousness and our childhood fears of the dark and of the horrible things that might lurk therein. Yet, it takes very little to awaken our dormant terror. We like to think that with modern education and an advanced culture we have left behind our old superstitions, but the slightest brush with the unknown still makes our hair stand on end.

The college son of one of our office secretaries had to write a term paper on demon possession for his psychology class. At that time, the theatrical film *The Exorcist* had just been released to the public, and the whole subject of demonology had captured the minds of our society. The boy sat up late to write his paper long after the family had gone to bed. At some time after midnight, when the lights were low and the house was quiet, a bird suddenly flew down the fireplace chimney! Those of us who heard the story the next day are still trying to imagine the subsequent scene as a frenzied young man chased a frightened bird all over the house and half-awakened people came questioning out of the dark bedrooms.

Yes, our tolerance for eerie coincidence is very low indeed. Perhaps it is because in spite of our attempts to rationalize every event around us we yet know subconsciously that the world of spirit really does exist. Human superstitions abound, but beyond this level of imagination there is a dimension of spirit that is independent of human invention. We cannot read the Bible without coming to the conclusion that there are evil powers that are not generated by the human mind, but exist in their own paraphysical cosmos. Jesus recognized the existence of the devil and his hosts of demonic spirits. In fact, theologians are still bothered by the apparent frequency with which He encountered these dark powers. Perhaps we have not yet become sufficiently acquainted with the spirit world to realize how active are the forces of good and evil just beyond the sensitivity limits of man.

The late 20th century has seen a revival of interest in extrasensory phenomena and the occult. In a number of universities there are studies in progress on a wide range of paraphysical subjects, including the interpretation of dreams and the determination of a personal aura—an energy field that is thought to surround each living thing or object. A great many experiments are going on to investigate extrasensory perception and other suspected powers of the human mind.

It is my observation from my missionary experience in the jungles of South America and in briefer encounters with primitive peoples in Africa that the movement of man toward civilization has not all been upward. Civilization simplifies human life by regulating it. As man structures his society, he depends less and less on interpersonal relationships and more on relationships based on predetermined social policy. Many of the powers of the human mind were developed and only may operate effectively within a fairly closed social system. Such mental capabilities as telepathy become lost once the sensitive persons move out of the society in which they have been engaged in a sort of group consciousness.

I used to marvel at the extrasensory powers of the jungle people of Sarare, an area along the Arauca River east of the Andes Mountains and on both sides of the border between Colombia and Venezuela. I had no way of telling them when I was coming to visit them; and yet I would fly for two hours on a commercial airline, go another four hours by inter-city taxi, spend the night in the town of Pamplona, take an eleven-hour bus ride over the Andes and down to the Orinoco Basin, walk on jungle trails for another three hours, cross the Arauca River in a dugout canoe, and walk another couple of hours . . . and find people from all over Sarare sitting and waiting for me! I would ask them how they knew I was coming, and they would just say, "Oh, we knew you would be here today."

It is my opinion that such powers are well within the natural capabilities of man, but that civilization has dulled the human senses. As we have lost our early abilities, we have replaced them with mechanical and electronic devices. To regain our former awareness, we would have to return to some form of group-consciousness culture such as that of a clan or tribe. Unfortunately, the tendency today is in the opposite direction toward a socialistic regulation of man into one popular culture. The church has always taught that there was a prehistoric fall of man. Perhaps we should recognize that the fall of Adam was even greater than anything we have yet imagined, and that civilized man is still falling farther and farther from his original glory, his trail of material artifacts from stone tools to electronic gadgets marking the slow increase in material crutches to replace his declining mental abilities. Such powers of the mind are not necessarily evil, although they may be warped into wicked use. They are a manifestation of what sets men apart from the rest of the life on this planet, and originated with the creation of God.

The current emphasis on extrasensory phenomena not only has revived interest in the powers of the mind, but also has reawakened the latent preoccupation with the occult—the hidden powers beyond the natural abilities of man.

Belief in astrology is certainly on the rise. The fundamental concepts that human personality and destiny can be influenced by the relative positions of the celestial bodies does not seem to be rational. However, certain personality types do appear to correspond to birth months, and some astrologers have been quite accurate in their predictions. The great problem with astrology for the Christian believer is that this rather mathematical art originates in pagan beliefs and practices associated with evil powers.

The Bible never says that astrology does not work. The first chapter of Genesis says the sun, moon, and stars were created for signs, as well as for "seasons, and for days, and years" (Gen. 1:14). The Bible says clearly, however, "Thus saith the Lord, Learn not the way of the heathen, and be not dismayed at the signs of heaven: for the heathen are dismayed at them" (Jer. 10:2). Although the Bible admits that one may learn to interpret certain celestial signs, it makes it clear that no man can master the field sufficiently to avoid being dismayed by what at best can be only partial evidence. The apostle Paul made it clear that astrological prediction cannot determine the destiny of a born-again Christian, when he asked, "Who shall separate us from the love of Christ?" (Rom. 8:35). He went on to state, "For

I am persuaded, that neither death, nor life, nor angels, nor principalities, nor powers, nor things present, nor things to come, nor height, nor depth, nor any other creature, shall be able to separate us from the love of God, which is in Christ Jesus our Lord" (Rom. 8:38-39).

When Paul said, "nor height, nor depth," he was using the Greek words for the zenith and nadir, the top and the bottom of the horoscope. He admitted that there are angels, principalities, powers, present and future relationships, the signs of the zodiac, and other created things; but he declared that the destiny of a Christian is outside the scope of any "principalities and powers." Can it be that the new birth reorients people to a greater celestial power, compared with which the basis of astrology is reduced to a mere game? It should be sufficient for any Christian believer to hear the Word of the Lord, saying, "Learn not the way of the heathen."

Today's occult revival goes far beyond astrology, for the ancient art of interpreting the movements in the heavens is only the bait that leads to a much more serious trap. An interest in astrological prediction often leads to other forms of divination more directly associated with dark powers. It is a simple step from astrology to the more potentially dangerous practices of reading tea leaves, palms, Tarot cards, crystal balls, and Ouija boards. Although some people acclaim the innocency of such practices, just outside their doors lurk the openly evil forces of spiritism, witchcraft, and satanism. Black masses are becoming more common in Western nations, and there are disturbing reports of blood sacrifices. According to the testimony of recent converts from satanism, there even are occurrences of human sacrifice in America.

The apostle Paul made it clear that the church is in mortal combat with the power of darkness. He said, "For we wrestle not against flesh and blood, but against principalities, against powers, against the rulers of the darkness of this world, against spiritual wickedness in high places" (Eph. 6:12).

In attempting to make our churches grow, we are not merely seeking to establish a success image within a growth-conscious, materialistic society. Rather, we are engaged in a spiritual battle against the powers of darkness in which the addition of every Christian convert to the numbers of the church is another cosmic victory. We battle against apathy, inertia, and our own limitations of vision; but we also battle against the powers of wickedness in that unseen dimension of spirit.

Evil, however, is only one side of the spirit world. The Bible says, "Submit yourselves therefore to God. Resist the devil, and he will flee from you. Draw nigh to God, and he will draw nigh to you..." (James 4:7-8). The secret of dominance over evil is the twofold action of resisting the devil and drawing near to God.

The whole purpose of the church is to reach out to earth-bound men and bring them into living contact with the reality of God. We must not forget the words of Jesus, that "God is a Spirit: and they that worship him must worship him in spirit and in truth" (John 4:24). The Christian religion, outside its humanitarian and social involvements, is essentially the dynamic contact of man with the Spirit of God.

I must confess that I would make a miserable materialist. Since the earliest days of my life, I have been surrounded by people with a spiritual awareness who when faced with any difficulty have spoken first with God and only then have turned to other more earthly solutions under divine guidance.

When I was two weeks old, my parents took me to a camp meeting to be dedicated to God. The Spirit of the Lord came upon the speaker, Donald Gee—one of the fathers of the Pentecostal Movement in England and America—who prophesied that I would be mightily used of God for the ministry. My father and mother took the prophecy seriously and raised me to be a preacher.

When I was about three years old, my folks were in a late night prayer meeting in a private home, and the little children were sleeping in the bedroom. Suddenly, all the children awoke at the same time and saw Jesus standing in the room. We went running into the prayer meeting and told the adults, but when they came back to the bedroom He was not to be seen. Still, I knew He was there.

When I was in grade school, my dad caught a large trout in the creek near our house north of Spokane, Washington, and my mother sent me to the stream to catch another one to complete the meal. I don't remember why I came to this crisis in my belief in God, but I looked up through the willow trees and said, "If there's a God, let me catch a bigger fish than my dad caught." It was an important test, because I had never caught a trout as large as the one I was demanding.

God must have smiled at that little, freckle-faced kid who dared to challenge the existence of the Almighty over the length of a fish. But He also must have known that I would need to talk to Him again over much graver matters. The manipulation of one fish must not have been much of a miracle for Him, but for me it was an earth-shaking event and the last time I ever have doubted His presence. At the first toss of my line into that creek, I caught a trout nearly two inches longer than my dad's fish. A quarter inch would have convinced me, and two inches were absolutely conclusive.

Since those experiences of my childhood, I have been in nearly continuous communication with the world of spirit. Sometimes by intuitive feelings, a few times by visual images (whether by physical presence or illusive vision I cannot say), at times by sending someone to deliver His message, and very often by the arrangement of apparent coincidences that lead to some purposeful result, God has spoken to me out of that mysterious world beyond the normal range of my earthly senses. I believe strongly that the zone of communication between the spiritual and physical dimensions should be the natural habitat of the Christian believer.

True Christian religion is not something we do, but something we become. Jesus called conversion a new birth, saying, "Except a man be born again, he cannot see the kingdom of God" (John 3:3). As a child is born into a world of physical sensations, so the child of God is born again into a new world of spiritual sensations. Whatever else the promise of heaven is, it is God's offer to take us out of this limited material world and give us eternal life in the world of spirit. Around such promises of the presence of God and His eternal rewards for faithfulness to Him revolves the whole Christian religion.

The truth is that man himself is a spiritual being who somehow fell from a former awareness of his own nature. His flesh is as all flesh, and his bones as all bones. He is a complicated system of tissues and liquids and chemical reactions, different only in minor ways from the other mammals about him. Yet, in other ways he is radically different from the rest of the life on this planet. In an important manner that no scientist has yet adequately described, he is a creature of another world. He alone of all earth's creatures looks up at the stars and longs for his Father in his other home.

Throughout history, man has struggled with the battle between his two natures. When his animal nature prevails, he is more violent than the most vicious of beasts; and when his spiritual nature gains the ascendancy he rises to heights of accomplishment and expression beyond anything remotely comparable on this his foster planet. He does not remember very well, but he never quite entirely forgets that "the Lord God formed man of the dust of the ground, and breathed into his nostrils the breath of life; and man became a living soul" (Gen. 2:7).

The spiritual Christian must ultimately become a monist in his philosophy. The idea of monism means different things in different fields of thought, but in a Christian religious sense I use it to mean a belief that all reality is of one ultimate essence—spirit.

God is Spirit. All things were made by Him and are sustained by His power. Therefore, matter owes its creation and continued existence to spirit. Although the dynamics of this concept are lost to us in the dimly understood creation and final destruction of the material cosmos as we know it, matter is not eternal. It had a beginning and will have an ending. Only spirit is eternal and therefore real. Spirit is not only superior to matter; it is responsible for the phenomenon we call matter. Ultimately, there exists only spirit. Matter is probably not very substantial at all—only the energy fields created by spirit and maintained in order by the infinitely consistent mind of God. This in a brief statement is my concept of the philosophy of Christian monism.

What does this mean for the average Christian believer sitting in the pew on Sunday morning?

For one thing, it means that any system of human values based on material gain is in deep error. The set of values for the true Christian will be formed upon a spiritual base. It also means that religion must be much more than the mere fulfillment of Christian duty. Every man must be born again to new spiritual life by accepting personal forgiveness for sin and believing in the person and work of Jesus Christ. It means a man must regain the contact with God that was lost to his primitive ancestors, and that he must maintain an open communication with God until the hour of his physical death and spiritual liberation. He must recognize that he came from that realm of spirit, and to that world he will return again.

The personal contact between a man and the eternal Spirit of God—the Source of all that is—is the most important concept possible to man. It is for this dynamic communication and fellowship between man and God that the church exists. God and man work together to convince a growing number of people about the true nature of the world and the true destiny of those men who will obey the Lord's commandments.

Reverend Thomas Lofton, a pastor in Phoenix, Arizona, wrote to me in a letter, "I strongly believe that the power of God is conditioned on human cooperation. There are three inbreathings recorded in the Bible. God the Father breathed into the first man the breath of life, and he became a living soul. The Son of God breathed upon the men who were His disciples, and they received the Holy Spirit. Then, the Holy Spirit breathed upon holy men, and they produced the Bible. In each of the three, there is something of God and something of man. The first man came from the dust of the earth, but his life was from God. The disciples were men, but they became the temples of the Holy Spirit. Men wrote the Bible, but their words were divinely inspired. God has always used men to accomplish His plan."

Yes, something of God and something of man. When men draw near to God, God draws near to them; and the result of that meeting holds the potential power to revolutionize the world. It is at this critical meeting place of God and man that the church lives and breathes and has its being.

Of course, there are evil powers in that spirit world, but they are of a negative kind, like shadows that cannot resist the coming of light. Compared to the real powers of God, the forces of evil are as nothing.

If a church is to grow in a New Testament sense, it must take advantage of the best in human administration, structure, and creativity; but it also must recognize its own spiritual nature and wage its battle in the world of spirit. At the vital point of touch where the hand of God comes into dynamic contact with the hand of man, the church welcomes its community and its world to its wonderful work of spiritual deliverance.

9

Cast Your Net on the Other Side

In an armchair in my office sat Cho Yonggi, the pastor of one of the world's largest churches—Full Gospel Central Church in Seoul, Korea. Only a few years before, the church had been the pilot project for a set of new concepts in foreign missionary evangelization. and now the congregation claimed more than 20,000 active members.

I knew the church was large, for I had written several magazine articles on the project when it numbered between 7,000 and 10,000 believers. I also was very familiar with the concepts upon which the church had been developed, and in fact had used similar ideas in my church in Bogota, Colombia. What I did not know was how Cho Yonggi had organized his congregation after he passed 10,000 in attendance; and I was very anxious to know if his church was still growing.

The Korean pastor sat with his hands folded in front of him, only occasionally lifting them to make short, emphatic gestures as he spoke. He was an amazing man, whose fluent command of English came as a pleasant surprise. A Buddhist until he was a young adult, he was converted under the ministry of American missionaries and was educated in the Assemblies of God Bible school in Korea. Today, he is undoubtedly the leading Protestant voice in Asia and a highly respected leader in many gatherings of worldwide influence.

My interview with Cho Yonggi took place in the month of March, and he told me his church had grown by 3,000 members since September.

I asked him, "How do you account for that growth?"

"Partly, it is because we moved into our new building," he said. "The new church will seat 10,000 people if we put some of them downstairs and use our closed-circuit television system. The building cost us five million dollars."

"Five million U.S. dollars?" I asked.

"Yes," he replied rather matter-of-factly. "Of course, we raised them all in Korea from our own congregation. We will have it all paid for by the end of this year."

I just shook my head. I knew the Seoul church not only had built its own sanctuary, but also had sent out foreign missionary evangelists and supported joint projects with American missionaries in Thailand, Vietnam, Paraguay, and other countries. I said, "To take care of 20,000 people, you must have multiple Sunday services."

"Of course," he said. "We have five Sunday services. But we take care of more than 20,000 people each Sunday. We count only the active, tithing members. This number does not include the children, who have their own services. Also, it does not include the visitors. Altogether, our attendance each Sunday reaches as high as 30,000."

My years as a writer and editor had made me wary of the figures people quote in interviews, so I asked him, "How do you count the people?"

"Well, we have tremendous records," he said. "Mostly, we can count the members because they all pay their tithes. It is through their faithful tithing that I can do all of this work."

It all seemed too good to be true. Cho Yonggi is a very inspirational preacher, but I knew he must have more than church services and accurate records going for him to be able to hold more than 20,000 followers. I said, "Brother Cho, tell me about your grassroots organization. There must be some secret you haven't told me yet."

He smiled and moved to the edge of his chair. "Actually," he said, "the secret of my church growth is the house meetings. During the week, the people meet in houses all over the city, and they come to the central church once on Sunday. Do you have a piece of paper?"

I reached into my desk and got him a sheet of office stationery.

"Here," he said, laying the paper on my desk top and drawing a rough map, "is my city of Seoul." He divided the city into parts and drew little circles within them. "You see, the city is divided into twenty-one sections, and in each of these sections we have many houses where the Christians hold regular services. My congregation meets in more than 500 such houses all through the week, and it is in those houses that people are saved and healed and filled with the Holy Spirit."

"Who leads the house meetings?" I asked.

"People laugh when they hear that I have 1,200 deacons. They just laugh. But those deacons are not 1,200 headaches, but 1,200 trained laymen. I send them out two by two to lead the house meetings. Every Wednesday we have a special meeting just for them, and I teach them and give them printed materials."

"So these deacons work directly under you?"

"Not directly," he said. "They work under my associate pastors. I have thirty associate pastors, and twenty-one of them lead the sections of the city."

I could not resist asking him, "What would you do if you were to start over again in another city? What would you do first?"

"First," he said, "I would begin in a house, where I would live with my family and hold services. I would go from door to door in the city and invite people and tell them about the new church."

"You wouldn't construct a building first?"

"Oh, no! You first must have people. As soon as I had a few believers, I would train them and send them out two by two to hold services in the houses of the members. We would start having more than one service in the central house as soon as the number became too large for a single service. I would hold training classes for the deacons, and soon we would be growing into the hundreds. After that, it would just be a matter of doing the same things we are doing in Seoul today."

I said, "It all seems so mathematical."

"It is like the division of living cells," he said. "It just keeps growing and dividing and growing and dividing. Of course, you have to preach a message of deliverance from sin and from all kinds of problems. People come to meet with God and leave their problems with Him."

I looked at the Korean pastor and asked, "Brother Cho, how large will your church grow?"

He said, "It will never stop growing. No church must ever stop growing, no matter how big it becomes."

The growth of Seoul's Full Gospel Central Church may be a unique event brought about by a gifted man within an unusual culture. Or, is it? Cho Yonggi says no. He claims no singular gift, but says that anyone can do what he has done if he will believe God for it and use this house-meeting method. I suppose we will not know for sure until more congregations try this approach.

The evangelization of the world is too important a task not to speculate on alternative ways of doing things and not to experiment with new methods as they are developed. We must be responsible servants of the Lord who will not do anything to bring harm to God's people or put their personal salvation in jeopardy; but neither must we remain paralyzed by fear of change while important opportunities and decisive challenges pass us by. The worst thing that can happen to a congregation is to become trapped in the cage of tradition; for the church was meant to be a liberating force in the world, creative in its ideas and fervent in its inspired action. A too rigid respect for tradition or a fear of change will limit the development of the church and keep it in permanent captivity.

When the Lord's disciples went fishing in the Sea of Galilee, Jesus stood on the shore and asked if they had caught anything. They were rather discouraged with the results of their efforts, for they had fished all night and caught nothing. As former professional fishermen, they knew that they had used the best of human knowledge and yet had produced no tangible results. How similar was their plight to that of many a modern congregation!

Jesus said, "Cast your net on the other side!"

What a strange request it was! No good Galilean fisherman would want to be seen pulling up his nets only to cast them on the other side of the boat. Generations of fishermen over many centuries always had managed their nets in the same traditional way. What difference could it possibly make to cast the net on the other side?

Fortunately, the disciples already had learned not to question the creative uniqueness of their Master. Nothing else had worked for them that night. Why should they not try some alternative solution to their problem, even if it did seem embarrassingly bizarre?

No sooner had they tried out the peculiar idea than their net was suddenly filled with thousands of flailing fish. So great was the catch that the net began to break, and it was only with great difficulty that they brought their fish to shore.

How often I have heard the old-time preachers say, "When you come to the end of your rope, let go and let God have His way." When traditional human methods fail to produce the desired results, we must break with the past and speculate on alternative means. And, along with our creative experimentation, we must believe in God for a miracle from heaven. No amount of net casting would have caught fish that morning if had not been for the power of Jesus Christ. The secret of the Galilee catch was the combination of the willingness of men to try a creative new idea and the readiness of the Lord to perform a cooperative miracle.

Two successful ministers from Kansas City—Bill Popejoy and Clinton Vanzant—walked into my office. Both of them are such actively alert men, both with thriving city churches, that we covered a wide range of topics in our discussion. One question, however, remained with me to bother some of my nights and influence several of my sermons. They asked, "How do you see the church in the future? Will the congregational form continue?"

I have made some claims in my lifetime, but I have never claimed to be a seer. I am more of a guesser, a questionable calling that requires a maximum of research and a minimum of subsequent responsibility. I have refined my guesses to three varieties: intuitive, informed, and educated. Ideally, the factor of research moves the serious guesser out of the purely impulsive stage of mere intuition and carries him up through an ascending scale from an informed to an educated status.

On the question of congregational stability in the future, my guess is that religious structure will prevail. Although the churches have in their power to initiate and lead deep changes in the religious life of man, I do not believe that we should abandon the congregational form of the church. That is not where our problems lie. The group concept of the church as the Body of Christ is a source of great encouragement and comfort to many millions of people, while a less interpersonal format could ultimately produce a massive epidemic of loneliness.

Yet, the question of those Kansas City pastors ought to keep many of us awake nights. Although we may not agree with our noncongregationalistic critics, we still should give serious consideration to better methods. The world about us is in a state of constant flux, like the water in a moving river, and within that fluid context of change we must keep our vessel afloat and progressing toward its goals.

I see the successful church of the future as a motivational and training center surrounded by a wide range of religious activities, directed mostly by well-trained Christian laymen. Although I strongly favor the congregational form of the church, I do not necessarily believe in the construction of larger and larger sanctuaries to bring thousands of people under one massive roof. There are more practical solutions to the problem of continued church growth.

Let us imagine, for example, a church with an average attendance of 90. By some new insight, the church adjusts its program to a broader scale and increases its attendance to 120. The church building is filled every Sunday, and the offerings meet the financial needs. The people begin to talk about buying new property where they may have a nice sanctuary and sufficient Sunday school space. They manage somehow to sell their old building and construct new facilities in a good location, and by a miracle that often does not happen they also expand their vision for an efficient church office and a wider range of service to the congregation. Over the following four or five years, they grow to 250 in attendance. Once more, the facilities are overcrowded. At this stage, many churches grow to capacity and then decline again to their level of efficiency.

But let us suppose that this church becomes inspired again to expand its vision. The pastor and laymen have been reading books on church growth, and they decide their church can grow larger. They discuss their problems in study committees. They send groups of church members to visit growing churches and come back with fresh ideas. They add to their ministerial staff, reorganize their church office, improve their training programs, and initiate more lay evangelistic activities in the neighborhood. Once more, the church begins to grow, and again the congregation must build larger facilities.

Before long, the whole church is caught up in the planning of what is sure to become one of the finest church complexes in the nation. They borrow the best ideas from afar, and they construct their new multi-ministry marvel of modern accomplishment. They most probably will have to move the church out of the city to find a suitable piece of property in their price range, but the few people they lose because of the distance will probably find other closer churches to attend. The fact that they go into debt by hundreds of thousands of dollars is well worth the privilege of attending such a wonderful church.

No matter how unique the building may have seemed on the blueprint, the finished product will have a high-ceilinged sanctuary with much woodgrain and brick in evidence, a large carpeted lobby where many people may stand and talk, an office designed by somebody who surely never worked in church administration, a fellowship hall with appropriate kitchen and dining accommodations, a youth activities room, several series of age-graded Sunday school rooms, and the necessary restrooms. The sanctuary will seat 800 comfortably, but can take care of 1,000 uncomfortably for special occasions.

If the congregation has the vision to put as much planning into its administration and ministry as it did into its construction, it may increase its attendance to 800. If it grows past that figure, it will decline again to the comfort level of the people and the efficiency level of its organization.

What happens next?

Should the church consider itself fully grown and be satisfied to add just enough people to balance out the turnover of members who die or move away?

No! A church must never stop growing. The larger a congregation grows, the more it is potentially able to accomplish for Christ.

But what should this church do? Must it go into another building program for an even larger sanctuary? Will it move farther out into the suburbs to find enough property for a massive church complex? Does it have to pave a parking lot as big as a shopping center? Is there not some stopping point in the size of a sanctuary? If so, where might that point be—at 5,000 seats, 10,000, a stadium of 50,000? How much is enough? And who is going to pay the bills for such mammoth structures?

Most churches that have grown past 1,000 in attendance have discovered that there is a barrier of some kind just short of 1,200. In any sanctuary larger than this the pastor is physically too far from his people. Something vital is lost, and that loss—perhaps related to eye contact between speaker and audience—caused a major limitation factor. Although there may be some valid exceptions, most churches should not plan to expand their physical facilities beyond a 1,200-seat sanctuary.

This does not mean, however, that the church should stop growing. There are two obvious solutions. First, the church may voluntarily divide into two or more congregations, who in turn will continue to grow and eventually divide much as in cell division. Over a period of time, such a network of related churches could pervade the community.

The second solution is to hold multiple services. A congregation does not necessarily have to divide at the arbitrary number of 1,200, but can make wiser use of its facilities. Many successful churches hold two Sunday morning services in some workable combination with Sunday school classes. And, there is no reason to limit multiple service to two. A church with a large enough staff could hold continuous worship services and Sunday school sessions all day Sunday.

A complex with facilities for 1,200 in the sanctuary and another 1,200 in the classrooms could handle 2,400 people at a time, if it had enough parking space. A second service and Sunday school would bring the potential attendance up to 4,800. With other services and training sessions in the early morning and afternoon, the church could conceivably reach more than 8,000 each Sunday.

The main objection to multiple services is the large staff

such a program requires. Yet, the same expansion of staff would be necessary for any growing program. The larger a church becomes, the more volunteer lay help is available and the more ministerial staff the church can afford. The major difficulty is in concepts of administration. A congregation cannot grow larger than the ability and vision of its leaders to organize and manage its program.

Ultimately, in spite of all we may say about unlimited potential growth, few congregations will ever come up to their maximum efficiency within a construction-bound system. Over the next few years, we will see more churches number their people in the thousands; but very few will have more than 2,500, even less will reach 4,000, and but a handful will reach 6,000 or more. Like it or not, most congregations will have to divide into two or more churches to attain continuous growth within a building-related format.

Well, what more could we want?

A lot more. Jesus Christ did not tell us to go into all the world and build bigger and bigger churches; He told us to reach the people. I have come to what I consider an important decision: *The present concept of sanctuary-centered churches is not capable of fulfilling the Great Commission.*

There are two basic problems. First, church construction tends to separate Christian people from the very world they were commissioned to convert; and, second, church construction tends to limit the number of people who can be accommodated by a single congregation. The sum of these two factors of isolation and space availability is a tragic limitation of the church's potential effectiveness.

In the light of these conclusions, my interviews with hundreds of pastors and laymen, and my own experience as a pastor and guest minister, I offer the following alternative plan. I already had formulated this design before I talked with Pastor Cho Yonggi, and was very pleasantly surprised when I discovered how closely his plan corresponded with my own. The truth is that both of us were strongly influenced by our studies in first-century evangelization.

Any alternative solution to church growth must begin with the church that is, not with an imaginary church in some theoretical setting. If a church has less than 250 people, its congregation should expand its facilities and organize itself to come up to this level. For the purpose of the following discussion, we will assume there is a rather unlimited population of unchurched people and that the pastor and his congregation truly want to attain unlimited growth.

The church I see in the future has a high degree of lay participation. The role of the clergy will be to teach laymen how to evangelize their own communities and to create the conditions in which spontaneous evangelistic movements will occur. The role of the laity will be to preach the gospel, present an effective Christian witness in every human setting, and to bring converts into the kingdom of God.

We are talking about a very different kind of church than we see about us today. Present church buildings would be changed into motivational and training centers, around which there would cluster many congregational cells meeting in an unlimited number of private homes. At the core of the program there would be a well-organized staff of pastors, teachers, and administrative workers who would keep the system operating efficiently and offer continuous training for lay workers. Worship, Bible study, fellowship, and evangelization would all take place in the many house meetings, while a central program of motivating and training lay workers would supply the system with a sufficient number of potential leaders. I tend to agree with Cho Yonggi that the workers should be sent out in pairs. There would be no limitation to growth, no barriers to the total evangelization of the community. At the center of the system there would be a sanctuary to seat 800 to 1,200 people, and all believers would come to the main church each Sunday. In effect, the main church would be turned into a worship center and a lay Bible school. The traditional Sunday school would be discontinued in favor of Bible teaching at all age levels in the house meetings.

Basic to this approach is the de-emphasis of the traditional role of the clergy and a return to the first-century confidence in the potential ability of the laymen to organize and participate in a dynamic religious movement.

A widespread network of house meetings working out of a central motivational and training system would provide all the right ingredients for a great religious movement that potentially could evangelize the world. It would not be limited by expensive church construction. Neither would it be bound by the exclusive leadership of a culturally isolated clergy. The church would utilize its greatest earthly asset—its millions of laymen now sitting quietly in the pew and waiting for their marching orders.

A major question is: How can we get from here to there?

We certainly must not do anything to confuse the present church or cause anyone to stumble over our new schemes. The present church is a living entity with all the necessary capability to adapt to new alternatives. We can change the present church if we will introduce these alterations in an understandable and practical way.

A church may take its first step toward the motivational-and-training-center concept by establishing what I call the homogenous approach to Christian education. By homogenous, I mean that Christian education should pervade the whole church rather than limiting instruction to an hour on Sunday morning. When milk is homogenized, it is treated so the cream remains evenly distributed instead of rising to the top of the bottle. A homogenized church school will distribute Christian lay education all through the whole program of the church. This approach essentially turns the whole church into a lay Bible school. Instead of holding Sunday school classes only on Sunday morning, such a school would offer both elective and required courses all through the week with the goal of training Christian lay-workers to lead future house meetings. Naturally, we must offer age-level classes for the children and younger teenagers. By the time a young person is in high school, he should be offered elective courses with certificates for their successful completion.

The homogenous method of Christian education would encourage individual mastery of the Bible and related Christian subjects. The student would not only study the Bible in church, but would be asked to read and discuss it in his home. In the fourth century, John Chrysostom wrote, "Speak of divine things not only in the social circle, but in the family—the husband with the wife—the father with his child; and very frequently renew the subject. Let no man affirm that the child needs not be addressed on these topics; for they must be discoursed of, not only sometimes, but at all times" (*Homilies in John X*). Religious classes are important to the development of a child, but they do not replace the necessary parental instruction in the home.

If such a program of Christian education is beyond the ability of a single congregation, then several churches could consolidate their programs of lay instruction into one Bible training program for the similar churches in a community. In fact, the motivational-and-training-concept would work best with one consolidated system in the city. All the church facilities could be used effectively for classes and multiple worship services.

The next step after setting up a homogenous lay Bible school would be to initiate a more active participation of trained laymen in the church services. The active lay leaders should be taught and given practical experience in all facets of public Christian ministry.

Once such leaders are being trained, the church is ready

to launch its network of house ministries. In the beginning, the congregation could send out teams of members to hold house meetings on a nonservice night or in place of the midweek church service. There should be no conflicting competition between the central church and its house meetings. Little by little, the house meetings would completely replace all but the Sunday services and the classes in the central church. As the lay Bible school developed, the facilities of the center would be used all through the week for instruction. Anyone converted in the house meetings could take training courses in the center, where he would be prepared for an even wider outreach.

The changes would come about gradually, with a growing emphasis on worship, Bible instruction, fellowship, and evangelism in the houses and administration and lay-worker training in the central church. Furthermore, all the members would congregate in the sanctuary for multiple services on Sunday. Once in a while, the entire fellowship of believers would come together in a rented civic auditorium or stadium to demonstrate its progress to the community. The house groups would not tend to separate from the central body because the leaders would receive continuous training, assistance, and administrative management from the motivational and training center. Two responsible leaders would be assigned to each house, and they would be required to report and bring their offerings to a weekly workers' conference. No man or woman would be allowed to direct a house meeting in his or her own home. Whenever a group would become too large for one house, it would split into two houses.

The activities at the motivational and training center would include administration; an expanding operation of the training school; regular meetings with the house leaders; a number of committees assigned to community and church relationships, social services, foreign missions activities, and a wide range of coordinated programs; and the planning and operation of the Sunday services.

The motivational and training center would also provide a variety of youth activities. At some point, it probably would add to its system a youth center with a gymnasium, reading room, and chapel. Although not immediately religious in every aspect, such a youth complex would form a connecting link between the congregation and the unchurched young people of the community.

Such a house-oriented church with a core of capable clergymen and a large number of motivated and trained lay workers could grow throughout a community in an unlimited pattern of continuous evangelistic expansion. Every time a house would be filled with believers, the cell would divide into two cells meeting in two houses. The costs would be relatively low, considering the number of people involved, and the results would be very gratifying.

The principle is similar to that of biological cell division. Dr. Daniel Mazia, professor of zoology at the University of California at Berkeley, said, "Double or nothing. With few exceptions a living cell either reproduces or dies; the principle is so simple that no one has bothered to call it a principle. A cell is born in the division of a parent cell. It then doubles in every respect: in every part, in every kind of molecule, even in the amount of water it contains" (Scientific American, January, 1974, "The Cell Cycle," p. 55). If such a system could be removed from biology and brought over into a socio-religious context, we would essentially have the sort of church-growth program I have described.

There are other alternatives, of course. If you have some other answer to the dilemma of producing continuous growth and the eventual total evangelization of the world, then by all means you must investigate its possibilities. I do not ask that everyone agree with my conclusions or my methods. I only ask for a concerned awareness of the deadly trap in which the traditional church has become isolated from the world and a serious consideration of the combination of a motivational and training center and scattered house meetings as a possible solution to the problem. Jesus Christ commanded His church to evangelize the whole earth. It is obvious that some drastic changes must occur in the majority of the Christian churches if such a total evangelization is ever to become a reality.

The church stands in a massive harvest field with the golden grain waving ready in the wind. It is now or never for world evangelization. Yet, the church is tragically understaffed, it has built limited barns for the harvest, and it plans to reap the grain with antiquated tools. The situation is absolutely hopeless unless we can somehow get the church to motivate and train more laborers, move out of its limited storehouses, and take up more effective methods.

I still remember that vulture on the rooftop, that enigmatic scavenger who so appropriately perched on top of the church where I had preached.

The pastor of the church said, "I think he's trying to tell you something."

That the church was dead? No, we had had a wonderful service there only the night before. The congregation was alive with many fine Christians who witnessed for Jesus Christ within a worldly culture. In that church, men and women had come in living contact with the Spirit of God. Sins had been forgiven, souls had been saved, and people had been healed. There was nothing wrong with that congregation. Those dear people loved the Lord and would die for His cause if called upon to do so.

It was not the congregation that was dead. Rather, it was their antiquated method that had reached its limitation. The success of future evangelization in the city will lie not within the walls of the building, but out in the streets and the houses where the people are. Those dedicated Christians will need their church building as a motivational and training center, but they will use it only as a focal point from which they will pervade the whole city with their spiritual witness.

All over America and throughout the world, there are many serious congregations that have stopped growing. They want to believe in total evangelization of their communities and their world, but they cannot identify with the cause of liberating lost humanity while they themselves lie bound in the traditional chains of historical Christianity. So intently have they looked on the glories of the past that they have forgotten that God still has glory enough for today.

By presenting a new working model for the church, based on maintaining congregational unity while pervading the whole community with house meetings, I have called for a revival of apostolic Christianity within a 20th-century setting. I believe strongly that only by returning to the original concepts of apostolic doctrine, religious experience, practices, and priorities can we carry out the task that Jesus Christ has required of His church.

The future of Christian evangelization lies in a return to the methods of the ancient past, of which Luke wrote, "And they, continuing daily with one accord in the temple, and breaking bread from house to house, did eat their meat with gladness and singleness of heart, praising God and having favour with all the people. And the Lord added to the church daily such as should be saved" (Acts 2:46-47).

The Pyramid Principle states that for a church to grow it must expand its base of organization and ministry before it may add to its mass of followers. There is no church on earth that will not grow if its congregation will return to apostolic methods and reach out in faith for levels of accomplishment beyond what currently seem possible in the context of today's building-centered concepts.

We have not answered all the questions about church growth, but we have opened the windows of the sanctuary and let in some fresh ideas. If you cannot go back to the stuffy air of yesterday's traditions, then leave the windows open. There is a big world outside that for too long has waited to hear what you and your church have to say.